Voodoo in Sadr City
The Rise of Shiaism in Iraq

by

Boone Cutler

Bloomington, IN  Milton Keynes, UK

authorHOUSE®

AuthorHouse™
1663 Liberty Drive, Suite 200
Bloomington, IN 47403
www.authorhouse.com
Phone: 1-800-839-8640

AuthorHouse™ UK Ltd.
500 Avebury Boulevard
Central Milton Keynes, MK9 2BE
www.authorhouse.co.uk
Phone: 08001974150

First published by AuthorHouse 3/15/2010

ISBN: 978-1-4259-8678-0 (sc)

Printed in the United States of America
Bloomington, Indiana

This book is printed on acid-free paper.

Contents

Dedication

Written and Dedicated With Boots On The Ground By:

Boone Cutler

Tactical Psychological Operations Team Sergeant

Sadr City, Iraq

The term "Warfighter" accurately defines the people of a new era who serve the United States during this time of war against Muslim Extremists. Some of us may be known as Paratroopers, Rangers, Green Berets, Soldiers, Sailors, SEALs, Airmen, Marines, and Special Agents, but regardless of how we are known or how we serve or what job we do, in this era, together we are Warfighters.

Special recognition goes to all who have ever stared down a rifle from either end of a muzzle, while standing on foreign soil away from home, or who have put their lives on the line against an aggressor that tried to destroy America . . . you too are welcomed to the Warfighter club!

This is dedicated to all the Warfighters, past, present, and future, who didn't get recognized for all their dedicated work done outside the wire and had to take orders from those inside the wire, who made the tour harder than it had to be ... Thank you (and you know who you are, Airborne!). If the shoe fits, wear it. It was about the mission, and your hearts don't lie.

My personal thanks go to my family and the families of all the Warfighters who served at home and lived in constant fear of losing us. Finally, special thanks go to all the Warfighters who gave their lives serving our country. May peace find the families who miss you.

To all the families who lost loved ones and to those who helped at any time during this war since 9/11, because of 9/11, or beyond 9/11, and to all who have been injured or who were not able to come home with all the body parts that they left with, I pray that God, America, Iraq, Afghanistan, and the rest of the people you sacrificed for dedicate blessings to you dearly, forever!

Foreword

By Major Brian Wortinger

Instructor of Behavioral Science and Leadership

United States Military Academy, West Point

Part of what makes the war in Iraq so damned frustrating for the soldiers fighting there is that this is not what they signed up for. Many of us in my generation, spurred on by movies like *Red Dawn* and *Rambo*, joined the Army to kill Soviets. Fortunately, we never had the chance to do that, but we thought that here in Iraq was our chance to prove to our grandfathers that we knew how to fight. Unfortunately, in this war, somebody changed the rules. Suddenly, shooting was not always the most effective means to accomplish our mission. In the parlance of today's military, the non-kinetic fight became more important than the kinetic fight.

The author of this book is one of many Army leaders who I have worked with who are passionately trying to pursue an outcome to this war that is beneficial to both the American and Iraqi people. In reading this book, the reader will start to gain an understanding of the challenges, frustrations, anger, joy, resentment, heartache, and triumphs that the author and his PsyOp team felt while they spent their time doing what hundreds of thousands of U.S. service members have also struggled to do—bring about stability, Democracy, and opportunity for the Iraqi people in an effort to better protect Americans here at home.

While in contact with Boone and his team, I was able to learn many things about Iraq, Sadr City, Baghdad, the Iraqi people, and life in general. He was the first person to introduce me to the concept of *learned helplessness,* and as a person who strives to understand the motivations of the Iraqi people, I found that to be an incredibly powerful concept. The idea that Iraqis had to feign helplessness in order to survive gave me great insight into the psyche of many of the people in this country that had been ravaged by their dictator for over thirty-five years. Learning about this concept and several other ideas that Boone presents in this unpretentious text will give the reader a soldier's-eye view of the war in Iraq.

The overused phrase "winning the hearts and minds" quickly started spilling from the lips of our leaders as we entered our second and third year of this conflict. While there were certainly still plenty of opportunities to shoot and get shot at, the trouble was that no amount of shooting seemed to make things better. In open combat, we consistently defeated our enemies. Unfortunately, our enemies learned from their mistakes and began operating far deeper in the shadows. Swaying the population with a degree of well-deserved fear and religious rhetoric became the specialty of our enemies. In military terms, the enemy's Information Operations campaign was becoming effective in making the populace mistrust us and tolerate them.

While the enemy was running his campaign, we in the Army were scrambling to catch up. Never having a great love for the media, we were caught quite flat-footed by our enemy's combination of a very effective mass media campaign and local threats that drove his message home in each neighborhood. We were lucky, however, that out on the edge of our Army, mostly in Reserve units that we had to dust off and prep for war, we found soldiers who had the necessary skills, training, and experience to help our Army deal with fighting this type of fight. While the rest of the Army was quickly adapting to the new reality and learning at an incredibly fast pace, it is from the heart of the Psychological Operation (PsyOp) and Information Operations teams that the Army was learning the doctrine of how to counter the real threat posed by our varied enemies in Iraq.

For those who have been to Iraq, you are likely familiar with the differences between the "daytime truth" that is meant for public consumption and the "nighttime truth" that is whispered between confidants after the hot desert sun has departed for the day. For those who have not had the privilege of visiting Iraq, the author will help introduce you to this concept as he walks you through his experiences in that foreign land. Boone's PsyOp team had a great knack for determining that nighttime truth and ensuring that their supported unit's chain of command knew it as well. I have little doubt that the efforts of his team saved many American and Iraqi lives during their time deployed to Sadr City and Tissa Nissan, and for this I will be eternally grateful to Boone and his men.

While you may agree, disagree, feel pride, or get angry after reading the following pages, I guarantee that Boone is shooting straight from the heart, and only wants to help others understand his view of the challenges of living life as a soldier in Iraq.

Semper in Hostes!

Introduction

It's one large box of pain orbited by anger and confusion. The main hospital building at Walter Reed Army Medical Center is an ever looming presence that houses the angst of war. It's like a starship from another planet and I have metaphorically been abducted by aliens. How do others adjust from war to being here or even going home? Not long ago I was responsible for what seemed to be a universe of my own where I weighed who might live, which might die, who would get and who would go without. Now I'm here at the Walter Reed Army Medical Center in Washington, D.C. I'm just stuck. Alone in a room with nothing but my thoughts of a world gone that I should hate but I don't. Somehow, I miss the war deeply. There is no mission here at the Starship. Nursing Rum mixed with NyQuil has become my way of coping in a new world I no longer care about. This world doesn't seem to have the capability to understand what I'm talking about so I have nothing to left to say. I have an endless stream of intrusive thoughts and the core of my soul seems conflicted. I often wonder if I have a soul anymore. Is there a God for me anymore? If I were God I wouldn't love me. Not so much for the things I've done but for the dark heart it took to do it. I'm not proud nor am I the least bit ashamed. Maybe I should be proud because I still walk the face of the earth. I don't feel remorse for much and I'm not sorry for what I've done.

It's been said that a sociopath has trouble recognizing right from wrong and they have little regard for the feelings of others. Right and wrong seem inconsequential to me and I don't care about feelings, not even my own. Shouldn't a good Warfighter be a sociopath? We train to accomplish the mission void of feeling regardless of right or wrong. Warfighters generally are trained to stow their beliefs and the military calls it selfless service. On day-one in combat we might arrive with the beliefs we were raised with but soon we block out the useless beliefs and we live. That's when our perceptions about everything really changes. We survive the experience and lose whatever waste might get in the way and make us ineffective. We live for the mission and to protect the people close to us. Life stops being ours to live because life becomes the mission and the mission is everything. Nothing else matters. Having an issue with my beliefs now would mean I was not trained well enough to be a selfless Warfighter or maybe I doubted my mission and I'd have to judge my own actions. That's a lot to swallow, forget it. Some shrinks here at 'Starship Reed' refer to what I'm talking about as recovering from a Narcissistic Injury. Am I the only one who thinks the diagnosis comes from bullshit arrogance? All I know is I feel unworthy of life, however, oddly I'm not suicidal. I feel a strange unworthiness and general sense of torment most of the time.

Authors don't typically write the Introduction to their book last. I am. The book was written during my tour in Iraq. It's a compellation of scenarios broken down from missions and life while deployed in Iraq and conducting Psychological Operations more commonly referred to as PsyOp. Our team was sent to the Sadr City area of Baghdad to conduct Tactical PsyOp in April 2005. I haven't told a lot of irrelevant war stories because they all seem to blend together. Besides, my stories don't seem cool in a sexy kind of way. I thought long ago that war stories would be cool but after being in a war I know they are not; they are not just stories, they are memories. Some are painful memories. Maybe I was afraid to tell the stories behind the realizations I experienced. Most people describe their wartime experience as extreme boredom punctuated by terror. I don't. For me it meant mentally terrorizing my enemy and I stayed busy. As a PsyOp Team Sergeant in Sadr City creating terror meant using persuasion effectively to convince people to kill one another while trying to convince others that freedom was worth dying for. Isolating both groups was paramount. Generally, the education level and mentality of a person living in the slums of Sadr City is about the same as the average American twelve-year-old. With that type of an impressionable psychological mindset I don't know why we spent so much time fighting and not more time using those basic conditions to our benefit.

My team and I could influence most operations to further our psychological objectives after very short analysis. First we'd establish how information was passed then we would develop a message specifically for a susceptible audience. We used our supported unit's missions to simultaneously conduct psychological operations in our asymmetrical war environment and most of the time it was impromptu. However, sometimes we had planned phases for our operations. Prior to a raid in any given area we could go out under the cover of darkness and psychologically prepare the area by casually talking to a few adults. Basically we'd assess their desires and more importantly determine their fears. Eventually we'd promote their ability to take control of their own lives with persuasive themes specific to what they had told us. At a later date our supported unit would conduct the raid in the same area and undoubtedly detain someone. That's when a PsyOp team could disseminate a divisive theme to make militia members paranoid through the use of effective lines of persuasion. Without going into detail, the PsyOp Team could easily spread a PsyOp message through a few local kids by telling them 'a secret'. PsyOp'ers could quietly explain how a militia member helped plan the raid because he was secretly angry about something 'bad' that happened to a family member. This was an easy line of persuasion because typically everybody was secretly angry about something the militia had done. The kids would inadvertently "leak" the message to a couple of adults who would make it *their* message before they passed it on and that made the message credible.

Typically, after a few days or after we had let people out of the Detention Facility someone would most likely die. Using death furthered our objectives to divide loyalties within or away from the militia because it was a usable condition of the environment. Using the dynamics of psychological operations gives incredible depth to possibilities. PsyOp can often be the most effective tool used to deal with the enemy but it's sometimes sick and PsyOp'ers need to be willing to get dirty. If a noble person of the community was murdered we had a great opportunity to demonize the militia. We would use lines of persuasion to empower a grass roots movement of people to get them to befriend us and turn on the militia. If they murdered a militia member we would profess how the people were ready to stand up for change because the militia was weak and a new democracy could be strong. Either way, we'd use the conditions to influence attitudes to further our PsyOp objectives.

At some point it all stopped being guess-work. When it became calculated I sheltered my team from some of the effects. I didn't want them to have any moral dilemmas down the road. For myself I thought I might have crossed a spiritual demarcation line by using my God given talents for speaking and reading people in a way that was not pleasing to God. People were murdered. Many were tortured. I decided on a single concept to keep me grounded in the mission: "Do it now, deal with it later." With that concept I held my mind together, second-guessed nothing and did my job to the best of my ability without hesitation regardless of how dastardly it was. I don't know what it means to second-guess the actions or decisions I made in Iraq. It wouldn't do any good; so for me it's more appropriate to say living with all of it is hard to do. My ugly reality was knowing that the only way we could get our measure of effectiveness was by creating an insurgency to defeat the enemy's insurgency.

It may sound like a counter-insurgency but it was more complex. Not only did our group of 'insurgents' need to attack the enemy; they needed to have their own competing political goals so everyday citizens would have choices. To do so we had to capitalize on the fundamental prowess of Asymmetric Warfare and do it right. We simply didn't have the time to follow paths that had been tried and proven unsuccessful by others. Our higher command didn't always condone our methods nor did they understand them but they usually understood the necessity of aggressive action. Since they didn't truly understand, they didn't interfere much unless they were pressured by some other half-stepping nonsensical commanders. We could have used a bit more protection and a lot more trust. A lot less childish scrutiny based in ignorance from them not being on the ground with us would have been appreciated. Hopefully, long after America leaves Iraq the 'insurgents' we developed from the shadows to stand up against the militia will become a breed of patriots thirsty for Democracy and higher education.

This mission was much bigger to me than simply surviving my tour. I was not a great military leader like Douglas MacArthur or Chesty Puller. I never saved the day like Audie Murphy, Sergeant York or the guys on the Doolittle Raid. I'll also be the first to say that I didn't fight fair. Tactics are not centered on fairness. Tactics are about staying fluid, perseverance and getting the angle of advantage to defeat an enemy or win a battle. Winning is predicated on who exploits a situation the best. There is no such thing as a fair fight in combat. On whatever level we were fighting we fought to survive the experience and gain some measure of effectiveness. We constantly dealt with an Iranian backed militia that was trained by Hezbollah. Their goal was to deny democracy from the people that wanted it and bring shame to America through losing the war. The militia didn't need to 'win' any battle to win the war; they just needed to stand in the way of our mission long enough for American support to dwindle. They did everything imaginable and without reservation. The militia committed murder, torture, extortion, kidnapping and corruption of legitimate government officials. All of it was supported and ordered by the militia's religious leader Muqtada al Sadr. Stopping the militia was part of our objective so we clashed often. Ultimately, we determined the best way to stop the militia was to promote the Iraqi people's seldom seen movement and desire to eliminate Muqtada al Sadr with Iraqi hands.

Killing Muqtada was the only way to stop his madness before the hundreds he killed turned into thousands. We continually recruited spies, and identified hoards of people that were only loyal to Muqtada al Sadr while his people were watching. We also found a wonderfully honest nation of intelligent people who live under a cloud of misused Islamic fear of death. The Iraqi people know what they want but have been unable to express it openly and this book explains what our team shockingly learned. I hope to also show you how we gathered information; how U.S. Army PsyOp is dissected and how it can be optimized to stabilize our National Security. Strangely, I learned most about the Iraqi people through knowledge of myself.

So far, I've been here at the hospital for over a year and I still can't go home, help seems minimal because there are too many of us for the doctors to handle effectively. Maybe there is nothing they can do so they cut us from the herd. Then we wait for divine enlightenment or we bury the walking dead with the sleeping ones. I think about war more than I think of home. Maybe I don't have a home anymore. All the bullshit bureaucracy here feels more like purgatory than treatment. Maybe they know I can't go home because home is gone and I just haven't accepted it. I'm surrounded by the pain and aftermath of war in this chemical prison full of psych-meds and wounded. By now the anti-drama of the drama has become surreal. I see wounded all day long in waiting rooms and struggling to roam the halls in the middle of the night when they can't sleep. Last night I was roaming the halls and heard a man scream, "Fire"! There was no fire. I know what he meant; we all know what he meant. He was having our familiar and communal dream where nobody could return fire towards the enemy so all he could do was frantically yell, "Fire... fire ... FIRE!" and hope somebody's weapon would suddenly work and kill the enemy so we could live through another patrol. To me he's just another tormented soul trying to sleep. It's an endless revolving door of busted souls coming back. The full breadth of injuries I have seen inflicted on the battlefield end up here so I usually keep to myself in my room. I hate being forced to become intimate with injuries and pain that I've caused to others and had forgotten about. It's better to eat Top Ramen or Mac and Cheese that my parents send in the mail. Starship Reed defines the concept of retraumatization. Death just makes more sense. I'm not depressed. Death is just a logical way to stop feeling conflicted. I'm indifferent to dying. How did we all get here?

For me it started on my first mission and continued until I left. I remember agreeing to go on a petty little mission to get acclimated while my team was still in transit from Qutar to Baghdad. Myself and several other Team Sergeants from our unit arrived in Iraq early without our teams so we could get the lay of the land before they arrived. My first mission was simple. I helped pass out book bags filled with basic school supplies to some local Iraqi kids. It seemed rather low intensity but I was ignorant. In hindsight it was a good first mission and I'm surprised at everything I encountered.

The platoon I was with for that mission had been in country for about six months. They were a kind and caring bunch of guys who wanted to do something nice for the impoverished kids of Sadr City. Simple, right? I sat with the Platoon Sergeant and his Lieutenant for a quick down and dirty briefing about the mission. We cordially introduced ourselves to each other and made small talk for about half an hour. They were genuinely well-mannered men with a realistic sense of duty for the mission. They briefed their platoon, introduced me and we headed out into sector where we'd be working. Several of us dismounted the vehicles as the trucks moved slowly one behind another while we walked in-between the vehicles. The gunners would alternate their weapons from right to left while perched in the turrets of the gun trucks and provide our security. They watched over us while we gave book bags to the kids. It was clear why we had to continue walking; if we had stopped the kids would have become overwhelming and mobbed us all at once.

To control the large group of kids we'd throw the book bags far for a while then alternate and hand them to some kids close by as they tried to swarm us. Back and forth the crowd would rush far and close. Little girls were a significant minority in the group of children because boys were so vicious. They had to be tough and fight because the boys would punch them in the face to steal from them. Few girls actually tried to get in the middle of the action. Most stood looking doe-eyed at the edge of the crowd and we'd try to throw directly to them. They'd catch a book bag and run like hell. The bigger boys tried to get all they could for themselves as they bullied their way throughout the crowd. Some tried to make us believe they hadn't already received a book bag, they would try to steal from the others or even grab them out of our hands. We were in full combat gear with guns but that didn't stop them from trying to take from us. Imagine what big kids would do to smaller kids. I was amazed at the level of brutality these poor kids would go over cheap ass pencils and paper.

At some point the platoon's Lieutenant quickly broke from our tight group of soldiers. He was alone and chasing someone. I followed him believing someone had a gun or maybe someone got stabbed. A thousand things instantly ran through my mind. I didn't know what to expect. I didn't know exactly what the hell was happening, I just knew that since he broke from the security plan he must have had a good reason so I needed to back him up. Smack! The guy he was chasing hit the ground hard and L.T. put the boots to him. I followed suit in the heat of the moment and dropped down on top of the 'bad guy'. I pinned him with my knee and punched him in the kidneys and back over and over. He was on his stomach and tried to curl in a ball to protect himself and he covered his head with his arms so it wouldn't get kicked in. With every punch I threw I gave it my all. To my surprise the patrol kept moving and nobody else came to help. I called out to the L.T., "What's he got!?" After all, I didn't see a gun or a knife. There wasn't a blast from a grenade he'd thrown, so why were we beating him. The L.T. yelled back, "Nothing! . . . but he punched a little girl." Then he stopped kicking and I got my first look at the 'bad guy' I had been beating as if it was Osama bin Laden himself.

When I picked him up he looked at me in the face for a split second before he ran away. That was when I realized I had been beating a boy and not a man. He looked to be a very terrified fourteen-year-old kid. Holy shit, he was a kid and even though it was around dusk I remember the L.T. sweating profusely. He wiped his face with the dusty sleeve of his uniform and he said something to the effect of, "This ain't Kansas, Toto . . . that fucker would happily of killed us both if he had a chance." Obviously, I didn't go to Iraq to beat up kids. However, something ominous caused the same guy I'd met a couple hours before who seemed very normal and kindhearted to make the mental leap from a kid hitting a little girl to the same kid being a hardcore insurgent. So, we beat the shit out of him. It just didn't seem logical but it was only my first logically illogical lesson of many. The smartest of us learned to use our American born empathy very conservatively during our tour in theater. Lickity split we went back to passing out book bags with a smile and occasionally passing out a corrective slap here and there until that patrol was over and that was that in Iraq.

Question to Iraqi Citizen: How were you raised to feel about Americans?

"We were raised to feel Americans were the biggest enemy to Islam and we must stop them from doing what they want against Islam. We were taught to fight them in order to stop them from hurting Islam. We were taught to fight them by any means necessary. For instance, we were taught to stop buying their stuff since the Americans were not in Iraq at that time. We were taught to fight them even in the smallest ways. Saddam and his regime enhanced this because he also hated America. We were taught special lessons in school and made to repeat slogans and chants that were anti-American. The chants also included glorifying Islam, Saddam, and the homeland. I can't remember the exact words right now but I do remember many lessons and slogans being taught to me since I was very young. All my family was the same way."

If things never got stranger than that or if that was the last time I pushed some imaginary limit of morality I probably wouldn't feel so out of balance with my world back home. At some point during everything, actions and intentions stopped being judged as right or wrong and became a matter of effective versus ineffective. I once persuaded an insurgent's son to lie to his father over the phone and tell him it was safe for him to come home. We were waiting for him at his house and needed to lure him in to capture him. It might sound unconventional but it was the nutty normal for the time and it was done to accomplish our mission. I did it because unconventional thinking was effective. I hated the people we were fighting after a very short period of time because empathy was never an issue for them when they killed. I refused to allow empathy for the enemy to hinder my team or me. I never hated anything before that time in my life. I understand how that L.T. made the mental leap from kid to insurgent on my first patrol in Sadr City but who will understand me now. Is this what it means to feel damned to hell for the things I have done, not done and refused to feel?

It was not uncommon to stalk a specific militia member to locate and capture them. The Mehdi Militia is known by several names: Sadr Bureau, Office of Muqtada al Sadr, Muqtada's Militia, Martyr's Militia, Sadr Current, Office of the Martyr Sadr (OMS), or Jaysh al Mehdi (JAM). There are many spellings, like *Mahdi* as opposed to *Mehdi*. But make no mistake that they are all the same entity that wear different masks to carry out a self-serving mission of control and religious dominance. Out of respect for the Iraqi people, whom I adore, I generally refer to the militia as they do: "Jaysh al Mehdi," which means the Mehdi Army. The asshole that we were waiting to capture at his home was a high-ranking militia member and had killed a family while I was on the phone with a little girl in the home during the murders.

The young girl hid in a closet and begged me for help. She stayed on the phone with my interpreter and me during the militia's raid. I heard yelling and gunshots in the background as we worked to get to them. My interpreter kept telling her to stay hidden and calm. Don't worry, we are on the way and everything will be okay was what I told her over and over. Meanwhile an unmanned aerial vehicle (UAV) circled over the place being attacked as our unit's Intelligence Officer gave me Situational Reports over the radio. It was agony. Eventually she reported there was no need for us to continue because the shooting had stopped and her family was dead. I didn't get the firepower, soldiers and vehicles needed in time to organize their rescue. She ended the call and I didn't hear from her again. Her family was slaughtered and all I did was tell her it would be okay when everything was far from okay. If you have never seen people shot to death you simply can't imagine all the disgusting details like I can. I'll just say it's gruesome and nothing like you see in movies. I feel so angry for that girl now.

By that time in my tour I wasn't the least bit sad. Actually, I wondered if we still had sweet potatoes in our fridge back at the base because they sounded good and I was hungry. I pushed it out of my head because it was a relatively common situation and empathy was the mental enemy. I didn't want to feel sadness for more dead people that I failed to help. A calm rage came to me easier and easier as the tour went on. How the hell can a person come home again and integrate back into this society? Will I and can I? Why won't they just let me recover at my home? I survived eleven months in Iraq. At this point, my year in Iraq has now turned into being away from home for nearly two years. I just don't understand why it has to be this way. Life feels like punishment.

At night I don't sleep. Sometimes I go days without sleep and rarely sleep without hearing gunfire that wakes me. It started in Iraq. I'd swear the base we were on had been getting hit with the enemy's artillery while I was asleep but my team never heard anything. I'm not saying I would get up or react more than rolling over, maybe. I had a 'fuck the artillery' attitude. There wasn't much I could do about a blind, random explosion dropping from the sky even if it did sound like a freight train and look like a Volkswagen. I felt the same way about roadside bombs. When I was in Iraq nothing was spooky to me but now any feeling of concussion like an explosion or sharp crack makes me uncomfortable and I think living in this hospital has made it worse. Any non-deliberate noise can consume my attention.

Some people think I have a hearing problem but the truth is I hear too many things. I get distracted and miss what people are saying. When night comes I get amped. Realistically I know the militia is not here in D.C. but at night when things are quiet I have an insatiable urge to go outside and hunt them. Those are the only moments I'm not in pain.

I have yet to feel better after sharing my experiences in Iraq. Talking doesn't 'liberate' me. When I say I feel sad about finding several dead newborn girls left in shoeboxes that appeared to have been suffocated I don't feel just a little sadness. I feel incredible anger. All of them had smashed noses and petequial hemorrhages in their eyes. There were about fifteen children altogether and twelve were girls. None of the little boys had smashed noses or broken blood vessels in their eyes. One might think I'd feel bad enough to scream or hit a wall to vent my emotions but that would be nothing. I'd have to hurl my body into a concrete wall until my bones were mush just to start to disperse some of the angry energy that I have in me about those babies. I know everybody wants to know what it's like to kill someone. Killing is not very hard but waiting with a mutilated human being and watching them die really sucks. People simply do not look like the enemy when they're bleeding to death. I feel somewhat guilty for giving them so much respect. However, not so guilty that I would trade places with them and let someone kill me. Kill or be killed is a very true reality of war. Either you've done it and know you can do it or you haven't; either you know what it means or you don't. It's easy to say but impossible to explain.

Strangely I sincerely miss the people of Sadr City and even wonder if they ever think about me. When people ask where I'm from my first thought is always, "Sadr City" and I don't know why.

Dealing with pain has been interesting. Since I've been here at the Starship I've felt a lot of it. It's worse than it ever was in country. About three or four months after I arrived in Iraq I was running across the base during a mortar attack when a mortar round exploded too close for comfort. For a moment I thought I had died, not as if I was going to die but rather as if I was simply gone and was already dead. I don't think it hurt me so much but I've had constant headaches and neck pain ever since. About two weeks after that I lost my balance during a raid and like a dumbass I fell on my head. I was seriously dazed for a bit. Maybe the earlier mortar blast had something to do with me strangely losing my balance. Honestly, I don't know and I've barely recalled the blast until recently and when it comes to mind sometimes I shudder inside if I think about it too much. So I try not to go there.

I wrote this book in real-time day by day as events unfolded in Iraq. The few dry parts are typically there to set up the larger view and perspective. This probably is not the best-written book of all time about the war in Iraq because I am not a polished writer. I'm just a Warfighter that wrote about my experiences during a war. However, it is arguably the first of its kind about Psychological Operations and Non-Kinetic Warefare written 'in the moment' of our Asymmetric War. I may change your perception of war and the people who simply partake in it versus the people who want to do it well. I might even convince you of a better way to fight because Psychological Operations is a dimension of war that is very rarely spoken about in detail or explained. None of the techniques are samurai secrets but few people truly understand it.

My information about the war in Iraq can be very shocking and may not be appropriate for teens, but that is a parent's decision.

Major Wortinger graciously wrote the perfect Forward for this book. He is a strong man of principle who teaches Behavioral Science and Leadership at our United States Military Academy at West Point. He accompanied our team on several combat patrols. He and I had not met before then, but simply by virtue of his job and mine, we became fast friends. His Forward is definitely the "prettiest" writing in this book. For those of you who have never been in the military, reading the way he writes and the way I write realistically shows how officers and non-commissioned officers (NCOs) communicate differently. They learn beautiful works of literature, while my poets tend to perform the music of Toby Keith and Mike Ness.

I didn't use a ghostwriter for this book and every word is my writing. Writing a book isn't easy and I might have never gotten done if not for the guidance of a talented writer named Stephanie Tyler. She encouraged me to finish. I met her while here at the Starship and she mentored me. This chapter and the Conclusion were written during my time at Walter Reed Army Medical Center. I've been recovering here after being medically evacuated from Iraq for injuries I'd been dealing with throughout my tour. After all was said and done it took two years and a Congressional Investigation for me to get released from Starship Reed. By that time, I ended up being away from home for three long years. I hope you enjoy the book and buy it for a friend. As you read the beginning of each chapter you'll find questions and quotes that display the general sentiment of Iraqi citizens. I hope this book provides what you are looking for; the first thing I'd like to offer is "The Warfighter Prayer." I said this prayer every day. I am thankful to God for His blessings and for all the people who were praying for me and the team while we were in Iraq. Here we go.

The Warfighter Prayer

*Dear God, please guide me and my buddies
with your strength to do whatever we must,
until our mission is complete . . .
Then grant us your mercy to forget what we must
and forgive us throughout our lives as we need it.
Amen.*

From The Shadows

Chapter 1

Question: Why did you become an interpreter?

"I like English and I felt that I was able to communicate with soldiers. It was an adventure for me at first because I was meeting new people and helping them to save my people. At that time, I didn't have to wear a mask or disguise. I liked helping Americans communicate with the people. It was a good way for me to get help for my people and I liked the money. My main reason is because I was exploring a new thing and helping my country. I absolutely enjoyed it in the beginning. It was the best thing that I ever did until it became dangerous."

I live in Iraq with my Tactical Psychological Operations team, and at times I am surprised we are still all alive. Should I get home, I might write another chapter about that, but for now, this is where I write. I don't know you, and few of you actually know me, but for some reason you are reading this book. It is not full of supporting documentation and cross-referencing to augment the information that I have to share with you. The book may become more like a long letter to a friend than anything else, and maybe that is what it is. Some chapters are only about how I read and study.

Here is the down and dirty: I don't read books or magazines that often over here. When I read in Iraq, I study Intelligence summaries, Situation Reports, and other PsyOp teams' reports. Incredible amounts of our PsyOp reports have been turned into Intelligence Reports. The reason that you don't see reference information to augment the information in this book is because I am the reference source. How can I use a news report to augment and support something that I write about when they are less comprehensive? My sources are the people of Iraq, my own experiences, and nothing second hand. I have conducted tactical questioning of the enemy, captured the enemy, and made my own discoveries that I have documented for you first hand.

There is a lot more that could fill volumes but I can't write about everything that I have known because it might compromise ongoing missions, and that would be irresponsible of me to do. However, please take what I have compiled for you and trust the reasons behind what I have told you.

At times, this book may read like an essay and I am sorry for the rare times it might run a little dry. Some places are a bit preachy but I really have done my best to simply be straightforward, and I hope you find a tidbit or two from me on my soapbox. I didn't come to Iraq to 'check a box', and there are a lot of Warfighters who put their heart and soul into the fight every day, so my preachy-ness is in essence for all of us that feel like I do. Let me get some of my views right out in the open; I don't like war, being in Iraq with shit that blows up, falls over, and shoots at me or being away from my home but it simply needs to be done. This is where I can do the most good and that is my obligation. I'm not proud to be a Warfighter,

I'm proud to be an American who simply is a Warfighter. I did it for my country, its values, and our protection in hopes that my kids don't have to fight a war that their daddy should have taken care of. I have made mistakes and tried my best to honestly learn from them and become a better Warfighter for my country to make my service matter.

There is a truth that I am going to whisper to you, and the truth of the matter is that there is a Muslim Extremist enemy that is very devoted to destroying America . . . "No shit"; but wait, there's more. Muqtada al Sadr is one man who is very powerful but he is only one of many, and Iran pulls his strings. Iran set up Muqtada in business to promote Jaysh al Mehdi for them to be used as a rear guard for Iran. This was to keep America busy in Iraq and out of Iran. Iran sponsored, funded, used Hezbollah to train, and did the planning for Muqtada to be successful. It became Muqtada's mission to keep Americans busy so we couldn't invade Iran, it wasn't his idea, and when that mission is over he will own Iraq from the shadows. I don't know if Muqtada doing Iran's covert terrorism is better than him acting alone as he gets more power or vice versa. Either way, Muqtada has an incredible amount of people larger than Hamas, al Qaeda, or Hezbollah, and they are eager to do their part at destroying us. This is a new Cold War, and the enemy doesn't fight in the open nor are they destroyable by killing. Killing the wrong person in pursuit of the correct person gives the enemy strength not only by increasing their resolve but it literally increases their physical number of fighters. Never has it been more important to properly target individuals without collateral damage.

There is not one country that is our enemy: Iraq is not the enemy, Iran is not the enemy, Syria is not the enemy . . . our enemy is only certain individuals in all these countries plus many more, but the enemy is not the country itself. They are a collective organization that shares an ideology, and it spans countries across the globe. The way we fight them is not with bombs unless utilizing a bomb will have a specific well-thought-out psychological effect.

This enemy is attacking the United States, right now, without even being here. Muslim Extremist are attacking us in cycles; first with an overt strike, and drawing us into an area to make us appear a failure by making us take losses (during which they reorganize and plan), followed up by their ability to accept their own losses and exploit our inability to accept our losses (even though ours are dozens or hundreds of times fewer). Next comes our own internal strife and our own populace encouraging us to withdraw. Meanwhile, we Monday-morning-quarterback the leaders of our Democracy for doing what we wanted in the first place; they are attacking us without even being on our soil.

This is why I say that Hezbollah is doing a better PsyOp job than they should be able to conduct; we the people allow them to do it. I know that I am not the first person to explain this concept and don't claim to be, but maybe I can make you more conscious of how the other side depends on it. They need this behavior from us to be successful and they look for the measures of effectiveness. Right now, they are happy with the body count but if the body count reached over 100 per month America would show their feelings, and if that didn't shake us they would kidnap us and mutilate us across the Internet until they hit a nerve. They will always up the ante.

Muqtada does not have the religious training to be named Ayatollah of Iraq, yet, and that is what he would need to run Iraq as the overall religious leader. If he had that type of religious clout or wanted it, then he would be more controllable, but he is young and very intoxicated by the power that he has now. If Iran tries to squeeze Muqtada out of the action, they will have to offer him another piece of the pie in order to appease him and keep Jaysh al Mehdi subdued. That is a very scary option for the future of Iraq and America.

For America to survive, we need to change. The military, the government, and the people all need to prepare our lives for combat because this enemy is not going to go away. We are not impervious to their methods; they can hit us economically, militarily, and covertly and, don't forget, with publicity. As a PsyOp'er I have a lot of ideas on how they could hurt us; it is just a matter of time and (with this book) I hope somebody with our government asks me my opinion.

I have spent ten months in Iraq fighting this war, and I have had enough. However, it is not over for any of us, and our best course of action is to realize that the enemy will use our strengths against us. Our Democracy, free trade, and freedom of speech will become their most effective weapons because we will not take the pain that it takes to win. All the standards that we once used as justification for killing other human beings and going to war will probably need to be re-evaluated. Actually, I am sure of it.

First off, forget going to war. If we "go off to war" like Granddad we are already behind the power curve. We need to "own" our threats before they become an issue. However, if we do go to war, the way we fight will be like nothing the military has ever done. Nation building will be our most effective weapon against the enemy. Building and controlling economies will become more strategically valuable than building military bases. First, however, we will have to invade the land, remove the government, and integrate with a new "plug-and-play" working government that will need to be in place longer than

5

the average American feels comfortable with so they can protect the infrastructure, automate everything that has to do with the cross-sharing of information, and give away communication devices to the people, while building support of the populace through the economy. Sounds like Colonization; it is, but it can't appear so.

We also need to conduct education modules for people to learn from while at new American-sponsored and protected facilities where they'll work and earn a paycheck to stay off the American dime to support their own families. The products and services from the facility should be filtered back into their own economy. We should avoid the appearance of impropriety by initially bringing in American businesses. Build universities to promote higher education as soon as possible to overcome the early anti-American rhetoric that they were forced to recite, which caused anti-U.S. fanaticism. From the educational systems will come the new leadership for long-term effectiveness and create the natural divide between church and state. We will maintain 100% surveillance by need, greed, and technology, and then target (yes, "target": that means "kill") only the "bad guy" and totally eliminate or come very close to eliminating collateral damage.

Iraq would have been a different landscape if we had done it this way. During WWII, a country's annihilation was considered total victory. But today, the world is different and we are smarter; besides, we are not fighting a country. We kicked the shit out of two countries because we were pissed off and vengeful. War for the sake of vengeance is wrong and a total waste of time. Look at us now . . . soccer moms aren't pissed off anymore; instead, they are fed up with our death toll, and now our resolve is shot to shit. Meanwhile, the war is not over and failure will inspire a hoard of attacks against us by groups we haven't even heard of, because they don't exist, yet.

The proposal that I am suggesting will control every plate of food and every dollar of every household. It sounds ridiculous but I am suggesting that we feed and clothe the countries of our enemies to protect ourselves. This "hearts and minds" concept *after* we destroy a county is flawed, it creates a Welfare mentality for the poor and makes it hard to sell the "protector" concept. We need total control by means of total nation building, and when everything is set, we turn it over piece-by-piece, but "maintain the keys," per se.

I can prove this because collectively the Iraqi people—smart, old, young, poor, and well off—have told me that America pushed a new government in their faces too quickly. We were more worried about being called "the occupier" than they were, and they knew that it was simply Muqtada's rhetoric at the time. We missed the truth; we looked at Arabs with American eyes and missed how they tell the truth. We were culturally ignorant. What they wanted was something much more basic to focus on, like industry and jobs.

We tried to do the right thing and offer jobs that affected public works by paying out big contracts to companies hoping it would "trickle down" and build the economy, but we didn't understand the corruption factor. That "trickle down" concept is an American thing. To put it plainly, we allowed ourselves to get straight-up jacked. It would have been better to have American soldiers control a work force that was protected on the job site.

This probably doesn't make sense, in our American minds . . . none of it does, and the sooner we get over that the better. I spent wasted time when I got here talking and saying things that were incorrect for the environment. I needed to get smart on the situation and that is what I am trying to pass on. We were teaching Democracy and freedom by the time the first Transitional Government was set up with an Iraqi face, and it didn't work. It doesn't need to make sense to us as Americans, just hear what I am telling you. We lost our credibility by trying to set everything up too quickly. That doesn't mean people weren't doing their best, and (in our American minds) the plan should have worked. Sometimes, things just don't work but that doesn't mean that we quit.

We are supposed to have American values, and quitting has not been associated with the American values I was taught. Now is the time to basically "put up or shut up."

The Iraqis simply had no idea of how to protect an ideology like Democracy that was foreign or fend for themselves but we (me included) just couldn't figure out why Democracy and freedom weren't flourishing after so many years of tyranny. Keep in mind that they were always taught that our way was wrong, and Saddam used our relationship with Israel to demonize us. We (me included) wanted them to have a quick operational government so we could get out before a well-organized illegal militia/insurgency bogged us down. We didn't . . . ain't that a bitch!

Believe it or not, they didn't want a government set up nearly as fast as we did; however, they told us just the opposite and in Iraq that was logical. The educated Iraqi people who I speak to think that Iraq was raped in this speedy process by unqualified American-appointed figureheads who are seen as thieves, and America has taken the blame for their malignant infrastructure. The insurgents have used it as justification to hate us. They wanted a better life and we tried but we threw a ton of welfare at them with no jobs. We tried to treat them as if they were us. We attempted to use motivators and influence factors that work on average Americans and it failed.

Now . . . jobs are not so important. I worry that we created a welfare country that will not take responsibility for itself but now, if they collapse we have a new set of "oh shit" circumstances to overcome. Who is responsible? We are, as Warfighters, first of all. Americans like to blame the government for failure and not want to blame military leadership. Our government couldn't react to anything that we didn't give them accurate information about . . . get it? Let's call it like it is.

I am about to say something that will make sense but only if you are widely open-minded: This is a Special Operations war that is being conducted by conventional forces, and with that comes too many conventional-minded commanders on the ground. The day of the total conventional war is gone, and we need to shift focus away from the history books. The kinetic fighting will continue on a situational basis, but the likelihood of a conventional war that we are used to reading about in our future is slim: Who could have a chance at winning against our technology? Unfortunately we have poor intelligence and information at the highest levels where nation building and strategy is conceived. Therefore, our non-kinetic fight has no teeth. So, our Special Operations need more command on the ground and a larger force for the future, or conventional forces need to evolve.

In no way, after seeing our level of psychological confusion, can I possibly believe that the Chairman of the Joint Chiefs of Staff, the Secretary of Defense, the National Security Advisor, or any of President Bush's administration is getting the info that they need. Special Operations forces are trained to assess and understand the things that are going on, and there are not enough of them in Iraq. As for the Tactical Psychological Operations team, we are few in a country that needs us the most and commanders are so "not accustomed" to us that half our job is spent PsyOp'ing our own just so we can do our job because commanders don't know how to use us or when to seek our counsel. We actually have classes on how to PsyOp our own commanders so they can be motivated to use us.

While in Iraq I had one battalion commander that my team was attached to and he was a "balls out" guy with good sense. Lieutenant Colonel Luck was a good commander to work with and he pushed company commanders and his staff to use us. As an organization, together we had a lot of success in Sadr City. I have to say, just as much respect was given by the previous unit to our predecessors.

Conversely, we worked for another battalion that we couldn't get much more support than a smile, and I believe Warfighters died needlessly. We could have helped. They just couldn't see where we were coming from, we worked at the company and platoon level but without the battalion support; it was like jerking off on a cow. Eventually, it might feel good but not much gets accomplished, you really look stupid, and you don't want to tell your friends about it.

The Iraqi people didn't even know what Democracy was before we came here to liberate them, and we expected them to accept something they didn't know existed, by the time we pulled Saddam out of a hole. We deserve the blame for that failure but that doesn't mean that we continue to fail; we have options. President Bush told us that it was going to take more time, and all he got was a lot of pressure from us (the voters) to make it happen quickly.

All the Iraqis wanted was to feel safe for a while, and at that time they were willing to learn. We were just as resistant to the war taking time as they were to accept all the changes at once. One might say that their problem was not our concern, but it is our concern because we fueled the Iraqi conditions for the insurgency by rushing things and not taking it slow enough and making necessary changes to the operational environment.

We the people put too much pressure on the government and created an unrealistic expectation that rushed to failure and caused the vacuum for the opportunistic simple-minded leaders and thugs, like Muqtada al Sadr, to gain an easy, unearned, external validation from Iran. We are pulling (have pulled) out too fast and getting what we the people unknowingly asked for. If the concept of "getting what you paid for" is accurate, we paid for a government to be removed and a government to replace it. We the people got what we paid for and won *that* war.

Now we may have to face some consequences if Iraq fails, and that is another issue entirely. We fought an unconventional war with conventional forces that were not qualified, God bless them for doing it . . . the living and the dead. Again, God bless those frustrated Warfighters. Iraqi Security Forces were corrupted as quickly as we put uniforms on them. We had the support of the people, but according to the Iraqi people, we lost it as soon as we vouched for the interim crooks that stole from them. Do you hear me whispering to you from the shadows of Iraq? Are you willing to shift your thinking, motivation, and support to stand individually so that collectively we have a chance to win this war that may take a lifetime? Our enemy is not only willing to do what I have asked of you, they outnumber us and believe it to be God's will for them to bring about the end of time.

Let's Get It On!

Chapter 2

After returning from a mission, Tactical Psychological Operations Team (TPT) 1412 relax and smoke an Iraqi water-filled pipe called a "Hooka." The Hooka provides a unique, cool opportunity to smoke "flavored tobacco."

Question: How is PsyOp different from other Army units?
"PsyOp has specific goals, and they try to understand the people and understand the way that we think. They look for opinions and the work they do is not for a short period of time, but they look for long-term solutions. They try to figure out the general atmospheric information of the people's attitudes in the area, and by doing this, it helps solve problems for the people. I have worked for four PsyOp teams and they were all different; some I liked more than others. Sgt. Cutler's team is the fourth team that I have worked for.

The first team I worked with had two main concerns and they were concerned with helping the people and determining what the political parties were trying to do. Some of the political parties were trying to find jobs and others were trying to find opportunities to keep young people from becoming thieves. For example, we had a good relationship with the Da'awa Party and they turned in weapons to us. That first team helped old Ba'ath Party members take a new oath to support the new Iraq. As a result, we got many weapons out of the hands of people that could have become used by insurgents.

The second team came in on the 28th of February 2004, and the first uprising in Sadr City started shortly after. They tried to continue what the first team started and met with leaders of the political parties regularly. The political parties were trying to get help to rebuild Sadr City and had plans for projects. We helped them secure their headquarters building, by building walls and providing weapons permits to their guards. In return, we got Intelligence information against ex-Ba'ath Party members and the Fadaeen. We were able to facilitate services in exchange for helping with the security situation and they gave us Intelligence information. At that time, the Sadr Bureau was not part of helping the situation in Sadr City. However, they were willing to consider being helpful to us at the time.

On the day we had a meeting with them, we went to the Sadr Bureau, but a member of the Sadr Bureau, Sheikh Hazeem al Araji, met us there before we went inside. He said that the meeting was cancelled because Paul Bremmer had shut down the production of the **Al Houza** *newspaper. The Sadr Bureau produced this newspaper. Because of this, the Sadr Bureau was no longer willing to be part of the reconstruction effort for Sadr City, and it was also the start of the bad relationship between the Americans and the Sadr Bureau.*

Soon after the first uprising in Sadr City started, the second team I was with could not leave the Forward Operating Base (FOB) much and was very restricted. Their efforts and the progress vanished. At times, we went out with patrols that we thought would not be shot at and attempted to convince them to stop the fighting. In return, the Sadr followers responded to us by showing us their hatred. From that time, I had to start living on the FOB and I had to wear a mask and body armor. It was the start of a very dangerous time. We even had to stay at another location to launch patrols because the routes coming out of the FOB were too dangerous. Other times, we had to patrol in Bradley Fighting Vehicles instead of our Humvees.

One day, the battalion commander's interpreter was not available, so I went with the battalion commander, Lieutenant Colonel Volesky from 2/5 Cav, to the al Jazaair Iraqi Police Station. We met with members of the Sadr Bureau. I remember Saed Kareem al Bukhati being there and doing a lot of the talking. I went with him to attempt to negotiate a peace settlement between Jaysh al Mehdi and the Americans. We told them that Jaysh al Mehdi must give up their weapons. The Iraqi Police would be responsible for the internal security of Sadr City and the Iraqi Army would be responsible for the perimeter security. I really liked Lieutenant Colonel Volesky because he told the Sadr Bureau that the Americans were willing to keep fighting but if they wanted to help their people, then it was up to them to make the changes. He had a very strong character and I admired him. The Sadr Bureau listened to him but they had some conditions. However, in the second meeting, he made them drop their conditions in order to achieve the peace settlement.

The third team that I worked with got here when it was peaceful. They helped with crowd control situations at a propane station.

14

They were very good with the people and they made the people feel comfortable. They were very effective at learning what was going on. Sometimes, they could be violent when it was necessary, but they were good. They worked very well as a team and they took turns running the missions. I liked working with them the most. We joked a lot and we had a lot in common, and we were all the about the same age. When we went on missions, I really liked it and bugged them if we didn't go out. Oftentimes, I stayed with them in their living area instead of mine. They also had a good relationship with each other. They were not the best at PsyOp but they were a good team for each other and myself.

The current team, with Sgt. Cutler, is always trying to be creative and analyze the situation. We always try to find solutions for any kind of problem and constantly make contacts with the many Iraqi people. We are good at listening to the people and telling them why we are here and what can be done to make the situation better. We negotiate constantly by telling them what they can do for us and what we can do for them. We would do better if the supported unit would allow us more accessibility to more people.

Much of the time, we educated the people to participate in the elections and freely select a candidate without being afraid. We taught the people the true meaning of Democracy and they reacted positively. Sgt. Cutler and I have been shot at a lot together, and we respond by finding different ways to stop the violence before it happens. Sgt. Cutler is the most serious team sergeant that I have had. He is the most focused. The first team sergeant, from the first team I worked with, tried to be like Sgt. Cutler but he couldn't because he was a beginner."

For those of you who don't know any people that served in Iraq, this book might be especially interesting because I am writing this for you while being deployed in Iraq. For me, the time here is 2321 hours (11:21 p.m. civilian time) in Iraq, March 7, 2006. The team and I had a mission this evening and finished the night by taking a picture of us all smoking a Hooka pipe together. They have all bedded down and hit the rack, but I wanted to stay up to read some Intel reports and work on the book that you are reading right now. I have been working on this book since December 5, 2005, while being gainfully employed by the United States Army as a Tactical Psychological Operations team sergeant. Mostly my team and I have worked the somewhat-famed area of Sadr City here in Baghdad.

I am actually writing this book for you when I have quasi-down time and in between our missions. I hope by writing this book, while I am here, you can not only see but feel what I feel as things happen. For those of you who have never been here or spoken to a Warfighter on the phone or by mail while they were deployed, this may be an insightful way to help you relate to a piece of American history from a "boots on the ground" perspective.

For others who are family members of Warfighters who died with their boots on the ground over here, you may be able to gain an insight or connection to your loved one's experience. If you are a Warfighter . . . portions of this book may cause you to get mad or sad or completely disagree with me because I had a different experience and mission; however, we both understand each other and why we can't talk about this place after we get home to others who were not here. Throughout this book, I have written about several subjects and provided information regarding our mission and how the enemy, the Iraqi people, Iranian influence, illegal Iraqi groups, and my government (to include our people) have affected our mission here on the ground. The people back home (you) have played a part in all these experiences even though you may not know it. For those of you who support us, I would like to extend my thanks of behalf of all the Warfighters. I don't tell many people here that I am writing this book, but strangely my buddies suggest that I write a book as somewhat a joke because I am considered obsessed with our mission here.

I voluntarily admit, without shame, to being obsessed with this mission, not obsessed with war but obsessed with doing what needs to be done to win and end it. This is why I don't spend my spare time playing video games or watching endless amounts of Iraqi-bootleg American movies that are sold in the local "Haji shops." When I read, I study the enemy, our mission requirements, my troopers, our supported unit's mission, and myself in order to have the best opportunity to keep my men and myself alive so that we can accomplish this mission that we sacrifice for. I look for enemy trends through data that I can get my hands on, but the most important information comes from listening to the words of the Iraqi people while being face to face with them on combat patrols.

Vertical and breathing is a good thing; I don't tell my team about some of the close calls, maybe I am wrong but that is the honest truth and they have enough to think about. Hell, I wish I didn't know sometimes, I really am trying to make this a worthwhile experience for them. I find my own solace in trying to whoop Muqtada's ass. We have seen a lot of death, and the carnage the enemy sends our way can be ruthless. A friend of mine who earned his degree in English literature has taken the time to read most of what I have written so far. He repeatedly hounds me to define what the book is about. Well (with all due respect), I'll leave it up to you to determine what this book is about. If you are still reading, you are obviously not stupid and you must be somewhat interested. So, just keep reading and make your own decisions.

Honestly, how can I know what part of this book will appeal to each of you, personally? Originally, I wanted to write about all the things that I didn't see on the news reports while I was on leave in October 2005 because the people I knew seemed to be in the dark about the successes we were having. For some, you will relate to the threat I see to the American way of life by Muslim Extremist groups like Jaysh al Mehdi (Muqtada al Sadr's illegal militia). Others might relate to the basic soldier story written by a soldier while actually in a combat zone, with all the feelings still fresh and the words sometimes painful. There are some who will appreciate a poem that my wife wrote. I left her at home to raise our young kids alone while I am here fighting, and you may share her sadness.

No doubt, many of you may be offended by my occasional harsh language and consider me an unskilled author and uneducated because of it. Those people are probably right; every word here was written by a man with slightly more education than high school, and I haven't restricted my language to keep from offending anyone. I don't think the language has been too extreme or out of context for certain subjects; I write what I feel, and sometime I write like I am pissed.

At times, you will read my unpopular habit of calling the people of our Democracy irresponsible and our government too worried about political fallout during the war, and I criticize some of our military leaders who micromanaged situations here to a fault and failed to adjust to this type of war. Make no mistake or assumption, even though I may have other opinions, as a Warfighter, I tuck them away and follow orders that are given to me. But when it is my call to give the orders, I do things my way. If you are looking for beefy warmongering stories to build masculine fantasies around, stop now and go get your money back.

For me, this book has become about individual responsibility and consequences for choices at all levels, from the eighteen-year-old high-school student who doesn't think that voting matters, to the news reporter or film-maker who taints information to support a specific anti-war or pro-war agenda, to the politician who defiles the efforts of Warfighters or boasts about Warfighter experience to build a political platform for their Party, to the everyday "soccer mom" who just wants the war to be over at all costs, or to the Warfighter who wants to keep fighting at all costs just for the sake of killing. As American citizens, we all have the power to affect foreign policy, believe it or not, and we share a common responsibility to protect our freedom and ourselves. No one is exempt from this duty. The decisions and opinions that we make and share come with an obligation.

I have written about the psychological war in Iraq along with all Muslim Extremists who will continue to threaten our way of life and our options. I don't think that we are in a Vietnam situation as much as others but I do believe this is more like a post-WWI situation with Germany. During post-WWI Germany, Hitler psychologically appealed to, and won over, the populace, then showed them the reason for their poor economy. In short, he had a scapegoat for all their problems; he was passionate and convincing. I have done my best to uncover what the psychological capability of our enemy is towards their own people and us and what their tactics are that I have seen.

Additionally, I have exposed who and what is driving their motivation and how our outlook towards the situation makes the difference whether we win or lose. This war in Iraq has been nothing more than the Iraq Campaign during the American War against Muslim Extremists.

Voodoo in Sadr City

Chapter 3

*Tactical Psychological Operations Team (TPT) 1412, call sign "Voodoo."
Here training on the close-quarters combat range on Forward Operating Base
(FOB) Hope, Sadr City, Iraq. Being out of the "proper uniform" was always
our favorite thing to do because you don't have to be special to do it . . . you just
have to have some sack. For us it made sense.*

*Question: How have you seen PsyOp teach the people in Iraq
about Democracy?*

"We told the people that they have the power to fix the problems by
voting for the right person. If someone was not properly representing
them then they have the right to vote them out of office. Voting and
selecting representatives was their constitutional right. Sgt. Cutler
used different speeches that were tailored for different people and
situations. For instance, if people had a problem getting help and the
DAC [District Advisory Counsel] members were not helping them,
then they could vote for new DAC members that would be helpful. I

have seen Sgt. Cutler use approximately thirty different speeches to teach people about Democracy."

Voodoo was our call sign. *Es mi Boone,* that's what I tell the locals my name is. We patrol the city with our supported unit, currently 3rd Battalion 15th Infantry Regiment of the 3rd Infantry Division (ID). There are four maneuver companies on our Forward Operating Base (FOB) that are responsible for the 2.5 million people in Sadr City plus the outlaying towns. Charlie Company, 2nd Battalion 22nd Infantry Regiment of the 10th Mountain Division is attached to 3rd ID here as well.

The FOB we all lived on is, ironically, called FOB Hope. I find it funny how it was called "War Eagle" and then it became "Hope." Either way, it was the FOB on the Northeast corner of Sadr City . . . who cares about the name? I think we should have called it "FOB Killing Me Softly with His Song" . . . it's sexy, yet sensitive.

1:40,000-scale map (estimated) above photo is much of Baghdad.

This picture shows a lot and puts a lot of terms that you hear on the news in perspective as to where locations actually are. You can see the famous Green Zone that is mainly bordered by the Tigris River; that is one reason it is felt to be so safe. The "big white box" is the Sadr City portion of Baghdad. People in Sadr City don't consider it part of Baghdad. I personally hate it when the news reports an event in Baghdad when I know it happened in Sadr City.

So, that is the nuts and bolts of who was there with us and what the responsibility covered. But this chapter is about the Tactical Psychological Operations conducted in Sadr City and the intricacies of Muqtada al Sadr's power. When it comes to PsyOp, I am not only discussing ours but also Muqtada's PsyOp program and how the things we saw in Sadr City affect Iraq and America. If this was a game, as an opponent he is very worthy, but it will be a different story one day. We influence the people's attitude in order to change their behavior to support our mission objectives. And for a time, we have, slowly and effectively.

In my American-raised mind, it is difficult for me to understand how so many people can submit to being completely controlled. There is a term in PsyOp that explains and defines the reason for their submissive nature. The term is called *learned helplessness,* and it is one of several cognitive learning techniques that we have to learn. In layman's terms, learned helplessness is no more than an emotional defense mechanism, whereby the captive has learned to submit to the captor's will and acts helpless in order to survive. Whether the captive actually believes in the ideology of the captor is not relevant because the goal is to survive and not challenge. The perception is that helplessness is their most viable option for survival. Iraq is a nation full of people submissively trying to stay alive.

Of the Sunni, Kurds, Shia (Americans normally refer to as Shi'ite), and Christians that live in Iraq all off them default to this passive stance when asked to do something proactive for themselves. Aside from the Kurds being gassed, Saddam Hussein and his sons were very cruel towards the Shia. Our team has identified that the majority of the Shia do not agree with Muqtada, and they are even willing to continually compare his brutality to that of Saddam. However, they don't have the ability to break from the cycle of learned helplessness that they learned under Saddam Hussein. We spent our time with these people and can validate that they know the difference between right and wrong, good and bad, and compassion and coldness just like the average American, but they lack the hope for anything different and personal know-how to step out of the cycle.

It has nothing to do with courage or intellect, and as much as we may think that it comes down to a personal desire to change and take charge, it doesn't. They have to learn from examples to do what they have never seen. American children grow up with stories about George Washington as a boy cutting down his father's cherry tree, "Honest Abe," or "The Little Engine that Could"; there are no stories like this in Iraq. But we taught them, we planted the seeds for change, and that was the nice work that we did.

Sometimes you use a carrot and sometimes you need the stick; we used both; either way, PsyOp seeds are very effective. There are many seeds in Sadr City waiting to grow. Quite honestly, I don't know if they will or can continue on their own without American support. But they are there, and Muqtada al Sadr doesn't even know it (until now, maybe), and he can't know where they are. Unless we continue to give them hope and support to grow, they will die because the competing factors are heavy and great.

Muqtada is a bastard and his death wouldn't have been a bad thing for our survival and some good people we knew that were being murdered. I don't mean a few people, I mean hundreds and possibly thousands in Sadr City. It was doubtful that any American would get the access to kill him and there would be some serious instability if America did that. However, it is possible to help influence others to do it. Finding the right person and motivation was very important. It wasn't like we were going to drop a leaflet bomb that said, "MUQTADA EATS PORK"; PsyOp isn't like that . . . not good PsyOp. The situation would have to be worked and talked through. Simply looking for the right situation and group without stating anything would take intense creativity and rapport.

There is a dual truth in Sadr City. There is the daytime truth that is inspired by learned helplessness that the reporters report when they stop in and get the quick down-and-dirty while the Jaysh al Mehdi stand close by. Second, and most important, there is a nighttime "whispered" truth that the people talk in the shadows amongst themselves. I have been privileged to see both and I understand them. Muqtada al Sadr may control what they say publicly but he does not control the truth in their hearts. As we learned the city, its people, and the influences that control them, I came away with extreme empathy.

It is the whispered truth that can stand in the way of his ultimate plan for a one-world Islamic government. The people love Islam, but not Muqtada's version, and that is where he finds himself living in a paper tower but doesn't know it. We can affect change if we are willing to back his opposition, which waits for our support. Right now, there are tens of thousands of people that wait for support. If we do nothing, then the whispered truth will only become quieter as he gains more control and power. Children will become adults and his influence will corrupt them into an entire generation of Muslim Extremists prepared to sacrifice themselves for his ultimate plan.

As a TPT sergeant, my duties double as a battalion staff officer and allow the opportunity for me to work closely with our battalion commander. Along with the duty and role as our battalion PsyOp staff officer, I have the opportunity to see the decisions and help implement them from a level typically much higher than my rank normally allows. It gives me the authority, point of view, and opportunity to develop decisions as a subject matter expert (SME).

There are two types of operations in this war, lethal and nonlethal; some call it kinetic and non-kinetic. The TPT's products and face-to-face operations are no different than artillery for the mind. The TPT uses nonlethal fire control in the form of messages and themes in controlled phases to exploit the enemy's weakness and disrupt their influence, and that is how we influence the battlefield for the battalion commander. We have several ways to use these fire measures and though we focus on nonlethal options, they oftentimes have lethal effects.

Conventional PsyOp prefers the use of key leaders as communicators to disseminate messages. In Sadr City, all the key leaders are bought and paid for by Jaysh al Mehdi, so we had to develop key leaders and small spheres of influence from scratch, house-to-house, street-to-street, alley by bullet-riddled alley, and sector by sector. Our task was to determine susceptible targets and develop them to pass on messages even if they didn't realize it, and then incorporate our messages as part of the whispered truth under Muqtada's nose.

Typically, it is not a good idea to snap photos at night when we were conducting our face-to-face operations. This daylight photo shows a pretty good depiction of how we work.

Being this close to the local nationals (many that are probably also the enemy at times) makes some people from our supported unit uneasy until they learn how we do things. For instance, behind me in the photo, I have one security man from our team. He keeps people from getting to my back, at the same time he covertly feeds me information through an earpiece in my helmet. The team members in the gun truck monitor the supported unit's radio and relay the relevant info to us who are on the ground. Our team machine-gunner also watches and can relay info into my helmet earpiece.

So, I never get surprised by things around me. The supported unit keeps their distance but does use their radio to maintain control of the situation. Our team, with just two of us on the ground and the interpreter, can make the local nationals feel close and comfortable and build the rapport that we need. Likewise, I feel comfortable with their closeness because the people incidentally block me from sniper view in the daytime while I am stationary. The other guys in the open have a plan too—but I'm not telling! We work as a team; however, we are made to look like two vulnerable guys "just talking" to people. Add the element of darkness to our missions and our target audience felt we were more vulnerable than they were. It left the door open for wolves and sheep alike. This was a huge plus to us locating susceptible PsyOp Targets.

In this situation, psychologically, we can create unbelievable "gives and gets." They give and get things by way of our techniques and never know it happens.

It is unlikely that even a good man would refuse to set up an improvised explosive device (IED) because the life of his family depends on him appearing faithful to Muqtada, but we might have been able to make him doubt the legitimacy of Jaysh al Mehdi so he would set it up poorly. We couldn't stop a call to arms by the Jaysh al Mehdi for the people to rise up against us but we might have been able to keep the people from trying extra hard to shoot us. These sound like small concessions; however, it was the difference between living with a close call and a cool story or being killed by a devoted follower.

We conveyed messages that Americans were their protector and that Jaysh al Mehdi was their captor. And the people believed us because we spoke the truth and we whispered with them in private while Jaysh al Mehdi attacked them in public with fear. No amount of Muqtada al Sadr's propaganda could erase the pain his militia caused but trying to teach empowerment to an emotionally castrated culture is like trying to teach dentistry to a boy raised by wolves. It takes time and it starts with the very basics. In late 2005 several Supreme Counsel for Islamic Revolution in Iraq (SCIRI) members from Sadr City tried to assassinate Muqtada al Sadr and killed seven of his internal bodyguards during the attempt. Removing Muqtada's sense of safety is valuable. No retaliation attacks against Americans occurred.

Who Is Muqtada Al Sadr And His Illegal Militia?

Chapter 4

Question: How difficult has being an interpreter made your life?
"In the beginning as an interpreter, my life was so perfect. I was doing the job that I liked to do, I made enough money to get what I want, I helped my family, and I was helping the people of my country. I really loved helping my people. I made $300 per month and that was about 600,000 Iraqi dinar. Then everything collapsed and it became chaos in my life. Instead of being safe and going home and not worrying about people killing me, I had to always look over my shoulder. Now I make $1,050 per month and that is about 1.5 million Iraqi dinar. The economy has gotten much better since the Americans came. They have paid me fairly by raising my salary to adjust for the cost of living. My close family knows that I am an interpreter and they ask to borrow money from me. I cannot tell anybody that I am an interpreter because I will be killed.

My hardest part to deal with is that I have lost my friends. I used to have a lot of friends but now I cannot see them anymore because it is not safe for me to go meet with them. We used to go together to smoke the Hooka pipe and hang out. We used to go to the arcade and stay a long time playing games, joke around, and just have fun. I have a lot of friends. Now, the only thing I do is go on missions and I spend time at the Internet café on the FOB where I can safely chat with people and meet them. Seeing my family is usually very tense and I cannot stay for long, usually only about fifteen minutes or so, just long enough to drink some tea. Six of my friends that were interpreters have been killed. I would like to leave Iraq because things are getting worse everyday."

Question: What should America do to Muqtada al Sadr and Jaysh al Mehdi?

"Let the government deal with them. That will give the government confidence in themselves. If they do a good job, then it means that it can run itself. I want Jaysh al Mehdi to be split up, and if possible, they can get jobs with Iraqi Security Forces, but only if they are willing to serve the government and not the religious leaders."

Question: If Jaysh al Mehdi is not split up, do you think they can destroy the government?

"Yes, they could destroy the government. But they won't because right now they control most of the government and they won't destroy themselves."

Jaysh al Mehdi, which means "the Mehdi Army," get their name by claiming to be the Army of the 12th Imam, Imam Mehdi. By whatever name they are called, they are run and controlled ultimately by Muqtada al Sadr or, as we call him, "Mooki." His motivation is not for his people to be free; his motivation is to destroy Americans everywhere and to stop Democracy in Iraq.

When America is gone from Iraq, he with his supporters will continue trying to attack America one opportunity at a time. They will corrupt the freedoms in Iraq that we fought for and left behind. He has the capability and the resources to be a thousand times more deadly than Osama Bin Laden or Saddam Hussein. He has quickly moved to saturate his influence into the legitimate government of Iraq and he is supported intensely by Iran and Hezbollah. In Muqtada's world, nothing is done without his absolute control or blessing. He has a combination of traits that lay somewhere between Charles Manson or Reverend Jim Jones—self-serving ability to quote God to hold people unjustly accountable—and Yasser Arafat's ability to bait and switch public and political messages, while in private, he runs an insurgency contrary to his message.

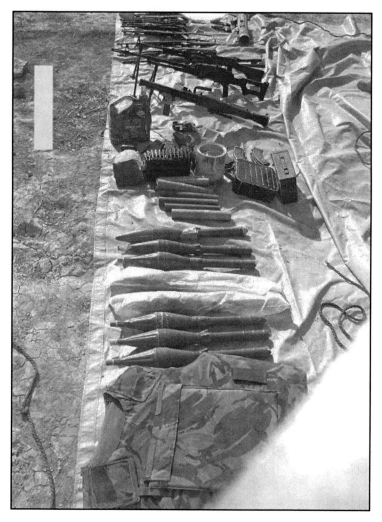

Courtesy Of: I.P. Gonzales

Jaysh al Mehdi, Punishment Committee, weapons cache. This confiscation was a good piece of work.

Muqtada al Sadr acts like a cult leader who hides behind the Qur'an and uses a twisted, self-serving form of Islam to direct special hit squads that enforce his will upon the people. If I had to pick one personality in history to describe Muqtada and Iraq, it would be

Hitler's influence and the Nazi Party post-WWI and pre-WWII. The rhetoric that Hitler used against the Jews is akin to al Sadr's rhetoric against America and Israel. The social and psychological makeup of the Nazi Party is very similar to the Jaysh al Mehdi, and rather than proclaiming Aryan supremacy to control the world, Muqtada professes a one-world Islamic government and death to everything non-Muslim. The difference is that Muqtada can use lessons learned from terrorist and insurgent acts of the twentieth and twenty-first century to further his plan and be very effective.

He doesn't need a technological war machine, like Hitler tried to do. Fear is his weapon of mass destruction, and should anyone be able to create and promote an Israeli type of security concern environment in the United States, we would suffer harshly. The Islamic Extremists could control many factors of our economy, and fighting for control of those factors is no different from fighting for the food on your dinner table.

The entire dynamic of Muqtada's rise to the top with his version of Islam and historical facts give him the authority to effectively dominate Iraq's majority of people, the Shia. There are many factors that give him the aptitude to wield a special psychological noose over the minds of his followers. He has the power and control over millions of people, and it will continue to grow and permit him to rule without consequence to himself. He is not a genius or a madman; actually, he is little more than an opportunistic cleric who filled a vacuum of leadership at the right time. However, the power he has might not only ruin the freedoms brought to Iraq; the factors he controls and that control him could pose a clear and present danger to the United States very soon.

The very name he gave his illegal militia is a symbol of prowess and potentially a key piece to his ultimate plan. Muqtada al Sadr will gain more credibility over time if he is not opposed. The cultural and psychological perspective of the name Muqtada gave to his illegal militia is very interesting and extremely important to understand what he might be leading up to and what he believes his role is in the future of Jihad.

Jaysh al Mehdi, or the Army of the 12th Imam Mehdi, is one of the ways he uses the Qur'an to serve his needs. According to the Holy Qur'an, the 12th Imam never died and is still living but he lives in hiding and will appear before the Day of Judgment to establish justice on Earth. This name by design allows Muqtada to validate the actions of his militia and establish future operations of Jihad to prepare the entire world for the Day of Judgment.

The 12th Imam Mehdi is the son of Imam Al-Hasan Al-Askry, who was the son of Imam Ali Al-Hadi, who was the son of Imam Muhammud Al-Juad, who was the son of Imam Ali Al-Rhida, who was the son of Imam Musa Al-Kathiem, who was the son of Imam Jafar Al-Sadiq, who was the son of Imam Muhammud Al-Baqir, who was the son of Imam Ali Al-Sajad (Zane Alhabedeen), who was the son of Imam Hussein, who was the son of Imam Ali Al-Mourtada, who was married to the Prophet Muhammad's daughter, Fatimah Al-Zahra. There are twelve original Imams or Guides, as told by the Prophet Muhammad, but this is the direct lineage of Imam Mehdi. The other of the twelve Imams is Imam Al-Hasan Al-Mojtaba; however, he was the brother of Imam Hussein and not in the direct bloodline of Iman Mehdi.

The Imam Mehdi was the last born of the original twelve Imams. The Holy Qur'an lists many traditions referring to the Imam Mehdi.

Most notable to understand Muqtada's motivation and Jaysh al Mehdi's ability to influence are that Imam Mehdi is going to come in the last days to make a universal government, Imam Mehdi is different than Jesus (the Messiah), and Jesus will be one of the followers of Imam Mehdi . . . Jesus prays behind him (Imam Mehdi). According to the Qur'an, Jesus and Imam Mehdi will appear at the same time, but Jesus will be the follower.

Taken literally, this would mean that the Jaysh al Mehdi and Muqtada assert Islam ahead of Christianity, and the American culture would bow to Islam under a universal Islamic government. Now putting it into a context of the modern-day Jaysh al Mehdi, we see how the Punishment Committee is used and justified in the minds of Muqtada's followers and conscripts. The Punishment Committee is a group of the Jaysh al Mehdi that murders, tortures, kidnaps, and extorts the people of Iraq. They operate throughout Iraq, but especially in and around Sadr City area of Baghdad. Even though he is known to reside in Najaf, Sadr City is used as Muqtada's command and control area to carry out these crimes in the name of his perverted form of Islam.

Jaysh al Mehdi enforces his wishes with the heavy hand of the illegal Shiria Court system. Those who know the tactics used by Yasser Arafat, how he was always slightly removed from crimes he orchestrated, can see how Muqtada does the same by publicly speaking out against atrocities, but in secret he sanctions them. He uses his illegal militia to control the largest portion of Shia in Iraq; he is slightly removed from the area but still controls it.

The Shiria Court is a religious court system that imposes sentencing on people for crimes such as the way they dress (people who wear Western-style clothes) or act in a way they see as wrong.

For instance, women who wear makeup, or if someone is seen as acting in a displeasing way to Jaysh al Mehdi, are kidnapped and then sentenced by the Shiria Court, much like the Taliban did in Afghanistan but more covertly. Everyone knows they exist behind the scenes, and their presence is always felt.

Just like the Imam Mehdi is believed to still be alive but is in hiding, so is the Punishment Committee. The people don't always know where they are but they do know that they and their informants live amongst them and are waiting to act. The Punishment Committee can kidnap anyone they choose, and then they will be punished illegally and without sanction of the legitimate Iraqi government.

When our Tactical Psychological Operations team was in Sadr City, we observed several bound, tortured, and murdered people. One time we happened upon females who were murdered, shot in the head after being publicly tortured on a street corner where sheep were commonly sold and slaughtered. Prior to being killed, one of the females, a young girl, had the muzzle of an AK-47 jammed in her vagina; then it was fired. This was a special torture the Punishment Committee used to send a message of terror and control. The girl who was tortured this way looked to be no older than sixteen. I don't care if you don't like reading about it because that is the way it was and you are not her, so count yourself lucky for another day and deal with it.

We were at the hospital near the morgue when the Iraqi Police (IP) arrived with their bloody, dead bodies in the back of their truck. We had no idea that the shots we heard on patrol a mere twenty minutes earlier came from the rifles that killed these women. The crime they committed was simply being females; the Punishment Committee needed to use them in order to make a point.

To cover up and try to justify the crime, the Punishment Committee left slandering notes on the bodies claiming they were murdered for being spies and prostitutes for Americans. I can assure you that the information on the notes was far from reality but the Punishment Committee acts as the enforcement squad for the Jaysh al Mehdi, which runs the illegal Shiria Court, and they are above the law.

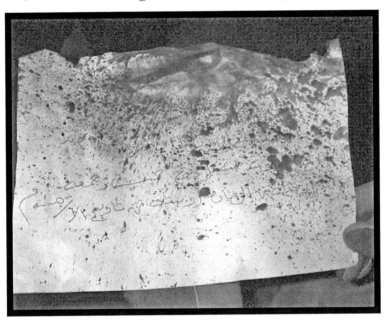

Out of respect for the female victims, I will not show photos of the women's bodies; however, this is a photo of one of the notes left by Jaysh al Mehdi.

This is a method used by Jaysh al Mehdi to control the people. In Sadr City there was little sympathy shown for these women after being labeled prostitutes, and the method ensured women would not help Americans by providing intelligence information about Jaysh al Mehdi. Women were a target audience for our team, so I took these murders personally, there were probably more. Naturally, this murder technique by the Punishment Committee influenced husbands and fathers to ensure their female family members stayed clear of Americans or they might suffer the same type of public murder and disgrace. The slandering information written on the notes and left on the bodies meant in this area of the conservative Middle East that those women were practically erased from ever existing.

Jaysh al Mehdi plays by no rules of honor that I can understand, then again "honor" per se is an American trait and we had to put that concept out of our heads. I remember that night as I was searching the bodies of the women for information and notes . . . I kept saying to myself, "'Dr. Phil' time later. Right now just get through it and get some payback." I swallowed my anger and sadness, I didn't show it to the team. I wanted to be a good example of professionalism; however, secretly I wanted to murder Muqtada and any Punishment Committee member that I could find.

The people knew the truth but they knew the point Jaysh al Mehdi was trying to make, so publicly and psychologically they accepted the crimes at face value. A few brave informants and citizens, who were there, without knowledge of each other, told us that these crimes were committed to make the people afraid to help themselves or provide information to the Americans about Jaysh al Mehdi.

The man who committed these crimes was one of Muqtada's Jaysh al Mehdi company commanders; his name is Abu Dura or Abu Derra; he ran a local Punishment Committee cell. As a TPT, it was not our job to try to produce informants, but because we pushed the right buttons and empowered people they chose to tell us many things that were helpful to our battalion intelligence officer. Producing spies and informants just seemed to happen; I thoroughly enjoyed getting reports about Muqtada al Sadr's main religious leader in Sadr City, his name was Al Suedi. Getting those reports was like crawling up Muqtada's ass and reading his mind.

It was our job to influence the attitudes of the people in Sadr City in order to change their behavior, and we did. Once we figured out how to approach and communicate with the people, it was easy to find people and allow them a place to vent their feelings and feel safe. They always wanted to do the right thing and help us but their overwhelming fear of Jaysh al Mehdi generally made them stop just short of taking action or standing up for themselves. In a way, the Jaysh al Mehdi was literally the "Thought Police," and the good people of Sadr City believed that Muqtada's men could read their minds.

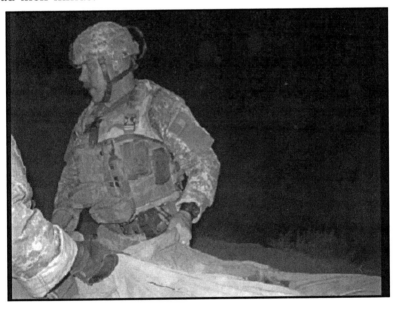

On this night, our team had the job of loading one of the dead victims of the Jaysh al Mehdi Punishment Committee into the back of an Iraqi Police truck.

There were many dead bodies found in our area. Time and time again . . . it was the result of the Punishment Committee and the Shiria Court.

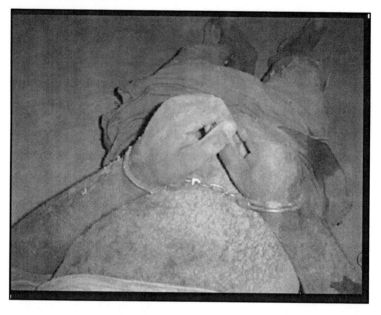

Bound, gagged, and tortured was how we found Jaysh al Mehdi dead victims. Typically, they were always eventually shot through the front of the head, not the back of the head; they saw the end coming.

The people thought that they would be tortured and killed if they talked to us. We developed several techniques and messages to get people inspired about Democracy and freedom; however, it was very difficult to compete with messages left by Jaysh al Mehdi in the form of notes attached to dead people. These are some of the factors that give him a more powerful psychological advantage than anything we could do. Stopping Jaysh al Mehdi was and is a job that will require Americans killing them and working as an instrument of the Iraqi people.

The Whispered Truth

Chapter 5

Question: How have you helped American soldiers?
"I helped soldiers by educating them on my culture and how not to take the wrong ways that make things worse or more difficult."

Our Tactical Psycological Operations Team (TPT) learned the best time to operate was at night. The people were able to open up more easily and absorb our messages when it was dark. Here is why: During the Saddam years, people learned that if they were invisible, they could live longer. During the daytime, there always seemed to be a Jaysh al Mehdi member close by and watching.

Regardless of what was said, whomever we spoke to was questioned and intimidated after we left the area. It just was not safe for them to talk to us, no different than the Saddam years. At night we could return to an area that we worked in the daytime, and the people would confirm the presence of Muqtada's militia. Nobody knows exactly how many of them were in the area; we didn't, that's for sure, but they always seemed to be around, or at least the people always felt them there.

If we spoke to small groups of people in the dark with a whisper, they whispered back. Yes, a literal whispering tone. With a whisper, they told us what was really going on. They also asked for help because they could not help themselves. The nighttime left less opportunity for them to be seen by Jaysh al Mehdi and less of a chance that they would be threatened for talking to us. They were simply more invisible and they felt safer. This was when the team was able to disseminate messages and themes of empowerment right under Muqtada's nose with less chance of them being countered before they got a chance to spread. It was definitely a little "cat and mouse" but the people soaked it up and they loved it.

Chesh and I were working a small crowd and teaching the importance of choosing a Constitution. Jaysh al Mehdi and Muqtada hated scenes like this. The people were abused for learning about Freedom. I loved having a crowd of young people when we could get them. They were proud and energetic. There were so many possibilities lost. Just look at them—you tell me! How hard is it to figure out? They were going to make choices and all we needed to do was create opportunities.

Taking turns as the cat is the worst part. No doubt the people we were generating as supporters were being killed, but if we didn't do it then our messages would cease. So, it was a true war of attrition propagated by information. If we didn't create enough people with free thought then change could not take place. And if Muqtada didn't kill them, he couldn't stay on top. I never asked anyone to actually DO ANYTHING for me, what they did was on their own.

During these whispered conversations, we could find out what messages the Sadr Bureau was disseminating and counter them. Whispering at night with a few people was more powerful and effective than a loudspeaker in broad daylight.

The men in Sadr City were consistantly happy to "vent" and "whisper" with us during nighttime patrols. Sometimes we left them with product to reinforce our message of how they lived in a Democracy where the people of Sadr City have the power in Sadr City and don't condone illegal violence against the people. Our team designed this campaign and the people loved it. Jaysh al Mehdi hated it. Our Product Development Detachment did a fantastic job and without their support we couldn't have left the signature impression we did.

I have seen glowing, positive news articles about "progress" in Sadr City that were great publicity. As a side note, I hate it when the Army Public Affairs Office puts out its version of "Information to the Public"; it is a "bit slanted" and I have personally sat in meetings and listened to embellished information put out on Sadr City that was bullshit. And if they call me out on this, I will fucking embarrass them. Them and this new-fangled Information Operations (IO) needs to stop trying to do PysOp jobs and just let PsyOp'ers <u>do</u> PsyOp. Back to the book: When civilian reporters typically did the usual stop in and ask questions, then soon leave, they never heard the whispered truth; I doubt if they ever knew the right ways to establish rapport, what questions to ask, or how to understand what certain evasive answers or body language meant.

We lived there, patrolled the city every day, and over time we learned their cultural ways and how to read them. But that took a lot more time than any reporter has to invest, and I doubt any reporter could even tell the difference between a member of Jaysh al Mehdi and a nonaffiliated local national (aka "Average Joe Haji").

One day, we were out talking to a group of people in a sector that was known to be pretty calm. We were only out that day to locate and analyze Muqtada al Sadr propaganda seen in new places by a patrol. I noticed that men dressed in all black were looking at us as we talked to a crowd. Wearing all black was common attire for Jaysh al Mehdi and their supporters. Besides, we could tell they were Jaysh al Mehdi by the way they were posturing and trying to hide but not hide their disgust for us being there. This was a day we could see a direct reaction to our messages and have a limited direct threat. It was like watching to see what would make your teenybopper girlfriend jealous at a party on any Friday night in high school.

There was no threat to the people because they could see that the people would not respond or interact but they were brave enough to listen to my monologue. The crowd grew to act curious but short of interested and so did the size of the black-clad men watching nearby.

We spoke loudly and were laying on a monologue of empowerment messages pretty heavy. We were telling people that nobody had a right to keep them from talking or thinking and that they lived in a Democracy so anybody who threatened them was breaking the law and could be put in jail.

Then something happened that was surprisingly overt: A Muqtar arrived and drove up to us as we were talking and stopped abruptly. A Muqtar is a selected elder of a community that is supposed to settle disputes and watch over things. He jumped out of his truck and advised us that we "were not allowed" to talk to the people. He told us that we were only allowed to speak to him.

This was a clear indicator that our messages were effective and divisive to Jaysh al Mehdi, but they were foolish and we had baited them for a reaction in order to see how effective our messages really were. It was the daytime, we were loud, and they never figured out that the real PsyOp was done at night with a whisper.

He acted very mad, dramatically self-righteous, and as if he was playing to a crowd. He was obviously sent to stop us. I doubt he was even the actual Muqtar because he looked no older than thirty-five and Muqtars are typically old guys. First issue, as an American, if another man abruptly stops a vehicle and jumps out . . . it tends to warrant somebody getting bitch-slapped but we had to remember this was a game that we started and did cause this to happen, so we used it. We used it well to demonstrate to the people, and that was always our intention regardless of however unorthodox it might have started or ended up.

He felt that his demands would be enough justification to shut us up and appease Jaysh al Mehdi, who were becoming agitated. There are few good ways to deal with such a situation like this and act in such a way to get the people's confidence. We couldn't walk away and do nothing. Nor could we show anything that looked like weakness, if we wanted the people to actually "buy" these concepts of freedom that we were selling and believe in what we were saying when we came back later at night.

I appreciate Jaysh al Mehdi showing us their cards that day and giving us such a great opportunity to actually mentor the people and show the people how they should treat a person who was trying to challenge their freedom by threatening them.

I grabbed the man by the lapel on his shirt and told him that I would talk to anybody I wanted, whenever I wanted, and if he didn't get back in his truck and leave that I would kick his fucking ass. I made sure, just like he did, that everyone could clearly hear me and see what I was doing. He left. Then I went back to my conversation with the crowd like nothing ever happened. This was not a schoolyard confrontation, and it was not done to display my personal overcharged male ego; I have other examples for that. This was done for the sole purpose of creating an opportunity that could be seized to show what individual empowerment looks like and that America was a protector of freedom while others tried to deny it.

The people seemed pleased with the outcome even though they still couldn't interact during the monologue. However, they smiled appreciatively and thanked us for stopping as we left with heartfelt handshakes and blessings, they actually winked at me when I said goodbye. The smiles and jovial response were pleasing. The people of Sadr City know exactly what to say and are always on the same page when it comes to public information. They know what to say and not do in order to stay alive. It would be unheard of for them to step forward and publicly speak of atrocities to a reporter or anyone else. However, that "wink" they gave me from their half-second locked eye meant the same thing in Sector 23 Sadr City as it would have on Main Street, USA! I was willing to do back flips for people willing to wink in the daylight near Jaysh al Mehdi because we knew the real deal. Believe it or not that was a successful daylight PsyOp patrol, it didn't get much better than that in the daytime in Sadr City.

They or their family would be killed if they spoke the truth, and there would be nobody to write that story or help them stay alive. The Shia people of Sadr City adapted to survive during Saddam by knowing the Party Line and sticking to it regardless of their personal beliefs. That learned behavior was a hard habit to break and Muqtada used it to his advantage. Routinely, we were told that the people wanted to tell us what was going on but psychologically we clearly saw them shut down and simply go to sleep and ignore the terror caused by the Jaysh al Mehdi. It was best for them and their family to stick to the story Jaysh al Mehdi wanted them to tell.

The best they could hope for was to be spared one day at a time, and talking against Jaysh al Mehdi would not make living possible. They would become another example of what happens to people who tell the whispered truth.

During Saddam's reign, the people became accustomed to a certain way of life. They became emotionally castrated over the years

47

he controlled the power, and they chose a strong foundation in Islam to soften the blow and find comfort. They accepted that they had little control over their lives and the only way to maybe gain favor was to support the regime. However, the people of Sadr City are mostly Shia, and the controlling party of Saddam was Sunni. The same mindset has continued through to today with Jaysh al Mehdi, except now they have some hope as Shia. Even though Muqtada abuses his power, he is Shia and that gives them some solace.

Sadr City was built by Saddam, the Shia typically congregate there in one place, and he made sure they knew who controlled them by naming the city after himself, Saddam City. Later it was called al Tharwa, then the people named it for themselves and it became as it is known today: Sadr City. But it was not named after Muqtada . . . it was named in honor of his father, Mohamed Sadiq al Sadr. After the fall of Saddam, they looked for hope in a Shia leader to be their deliverer. Muqtada stepped into the power vacuum as the leader for many Shia people. He was willing to be very vocal, he identified an enemy for the people, and he was the religious cleric with the clout of his beloved father's name.

Saddam assassinated Muqtada al Sadr's father along with Muqtada's two brothers in 1999, thus making him the only Sadr son, with even more respect because he is the son of a Shia martyr. Muqtada went into hiding after the assassination of his father and brothers. Only after we ousted Saddam was he able to come out of hiding.

Again from the psychological perspective, this was a great combination for the rise of Muqtada al Sadr. The people had been trained to live absolutely powerless and accept the mentality of a captive. Others were the disaffected and impoverished, who found a purpose in Muqtada's messages. Their only coping mechanism for their emotional survival was Islam and that helped this particular cleric gain favor. Unfortunately for the people, Muqtada was not afraid to use religion to control some and fear to control the rest.

Saddam made it easy for Muqtada because he had already created the conditions for the people to accept control from fear as a reasonable way to live. Sprinkle a little rhetoric about forming a militia to prepare for the Day of Judgment, where they will help rule a one-world universal Islamic government, and thus comes the making of a new terrorist organization consumed with world Jihad against all things non-Muslim.

Our TPT used several ways to influence the people in Sadr City (many of which I won't elaborate on because the war continues), but as I stated earlier, the most effective way was face to face under the cover of darkness. We learned to identify if the person or people we were talking to were a militia member, if they were an average citizen, or if they were sympathetic to the militia. Under each scenario, we developed ways to approach and influence them. At times Jaysh al Mehdi dress in their militia uniforms of all black or wear green headbands; the low-level members who provide non-kinetic operations wear canary-yellow collared shirts so they can be identified.

Generally, Jaysh al Mehdi members look like everyone else from day to day, unless there is a festival, parade, rally, protest, or a specific Jaysh al Mehdi high-profile mission and they want the Iraqi Police to leave them alone. When they are trying to blend, however, we noticed subtleties that made them stand out; they carry themselves a little differently and are consumed with emotion so they always gave themselves away. Again, no different than a cult follower, they couldn't help but talk a certain talk or walk a certain walk. The scariest part of this knowledge was being able to identify when the children were speaking the same language as the militia. This was the hardest part to accept. But it was and is reality.

Sadr City has approximately 2.5 million people and a huge population of children that can be seen everywhere. While on patrol, we visited schools on a regular basis. They are easy to find. Every sector has two schools. Saddam made the city so it is well mapped out in almost perfect squares or blocks, and each square block is a sector. Think of Sadr City as a very overpopulated, extremely impoverished slum.

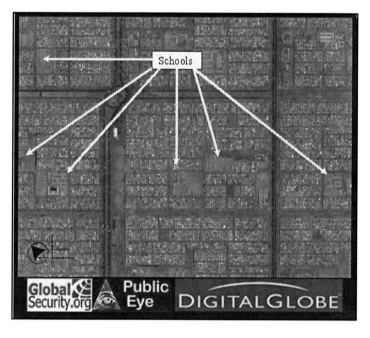

The center square above is one sector. There is a boys' school and a girls' school in each of them. All of the sectors of Sadr City are shown in the next picture.

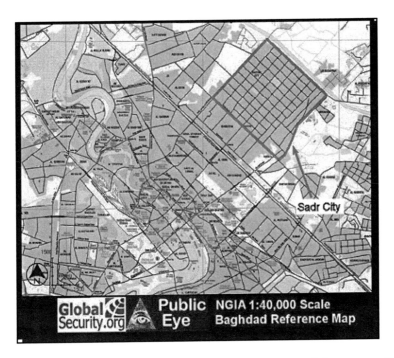

Above you can see all the sectors of Sadr City's approximate eight square miles. The sectors are bordered by the main roads of the city.

It is not uncommon for a 900-square-foot home, more like an apartment in America, to occupy between ten and thirty people, many of which are children under the age of fifteen. Saddam's goal was to consolidate the Shia, and he was not overly concerned with their comfort. The children go to schools that segregate boys from girls, and when we visit the schools they are often adorned with Muqtada posters, many of which are anti-American (Americans are referred to as "The Occupiers"). He does great PsyOp, no doubt about that.

Muqtada propaganda poster showing a child leaning on an AK-47.

Jaysh al Mehdi control the schools, where we have found weapons caches and propaganda cells. The guards of the schools are generally poor family men who need a paycheck; they often live at the school as caretakers with their family. The militia practically owns where the guards live and the family's income. Jaysh al Mehdi makes sure the children receive an education lined with information to generate the next generation of Jaysh al Mehdi. The children are just like the rest of the innocent children around the world, not much different than American kids in Texas, Florida, or New York, except at night their schools are used as staging grounds for militia operations like torture, transferring of explosive materials and weapons, or Jaysh al Mehdi meetings.

It would be hard to believe that these children were not being taught the things Muqtada wants them to be taught, considering we hear them speak the same messages as the militia and are taught to throw rocks at our vehicles in order to disrupt our military operations and movement.

Jaysh al Mehdi routinely gave children toys that looked real guns, and as they swarmed us with rocks they also pointed these guns at us.

It's common to have 200 to 300 children, under the age of fifteen, swarm our Humvees and pelt us with baseball-sized rocks. This is not playing; they become an actual mob. The militia uses children as pawns to try and provoke American soldiers to shoot them. When we first got there, adults would gather and then Jaysh al Mehdi would start a throwing fest with thousands of people, but Americans will shoot adults with very little fallout of negative publicity. However, shooting a "baby" who was "just playing" would create some serious backlash, and that is how it would play out for the benefit of our enemy.

Our patrols have been hit with rocks, bricks, circular saw blades, Molotov cocktails, and cans or bottles of motor oil, all thrown by kids. The soldiers of Forward Operating Base Hope are extremely disciplined and have literally taken it on the chin to keep the moral high ground and prevent several disasters. On patrol, all of us, me included, have all been tempted and would have been justified in most cases to shoot but kept the big picture in mind instead. Hats off to these young men of 3rd Infantry Division, 10th Mountain Division, and their attachments for doing a hard job and not giving Muqtada al Sadr the satisfaction of a propaganda war that would have been his victory.

The people of Sadr City have told us that the Jaysh al Mehdi teaches the children to do these things and then rewards them for being brave for Islam. They put a lot of children's lives in danger for the sake of trying to create a very bad situation. But they don't care about innocence. As a child, they learn to throw rocks as a game, then as young adult they can make the easy step to rocket-propelled grenades, improvised explosive devices, and AK-47s. There is a shitload of frustration put into conducting operations in Iraq but we do what needs to get done; it's not easy. And I'm just referring to the kids in this chapter. Don't get me started on the snap-crackle-boom stuff.

Tactical Psyop Today

Chapter 6

Sgt. Ed "Nacho" Keidis is shown here conducting mission preparation. It often started hours prior to the mission, which made for constant work. This man is as steady and reliable as the sun. For twelve months (an entire tour of duty), we didn't have anything break that kept us from rolling out the gate. He made sure that the vehicle, weapons, radios, ordinance, ammo, water, and an assload more stuff was always "mission ready" the way I wanted it and at the drop of a hat (poor him!). That might not sound like a big deal but when you are always getting shot at and driving a vehicle that wasn't made for armor in 120 degree heat, it is a big deal; I can be a real pain when it comes to having certain things my way! He is a phenominal human being. This picture was taken on another FOB that we were loaned out to.

Question: What ways do you hide yourself to keep yourself safe?
"I always have to hide myself to be safe. I met a new interpreter one time and tried to tell him what to do and he didn't listen to me, and he was killed the day after I met him. If I go out, I don't take the same routes and I always try to blend in with other Iraqis. I hide any U.S. equipment or documents. I don't wear the same things that I wear

on missions. Right now, there are many Jaysh al Mehdi checkpoints and one of the things they look for are interpreters that work for Americans. Realistically, they probably already know who I am since I worked at FOB Hope. I know that there is probably an interpreter that I know that works for Jaysh al Mehdi. When my friends ask me to pose for a photo, I won't do it because I don't want them to have an easy time getting a picture of me. Most of the time, I live on the FOB and I always wear a mask when I go out on a mission with the team. The road to my home is very dangerous to travel."

I had the benefit of being trained and working in other types of jobs in the Army, other than just Tactical Psychological Operations. I spent two years in Germany in the infantry, and in 1992 I was stationed with the 82nd Airborne Division. I graduated Airborne School in 1990, and it was only a matter of time before I became a real paratrooper and did my time in Division. (Paratroopers refer to the 82nd Airborne Division as "Division." The Army has several divisions of soldiers but to us the Army only has one Division.)

While in Division, I was first introduced to PsyOp by a staff sergeant who gave me a ride to the barracks following a school we were both attending. He had a car. I spent all my money on cheap beer and dirty women, so I needed a ride. As a young sergeant in Division, killing the enemy was our only focus; if I had written a book during that time in my life it would look very different than this because I didn't know what the non-kinetic fight was. We were typically young, ego-driven warmongers who wanted to find, fix, and finish the enemy by means of fire and maneuver as part of our Airborne mission.

I loved Division and everything about it. To this day, I still consider the 82nd as a second birthplace for me. It has its place in the military and I don't think it or the dedication and mindset of the American paratrooper can ever be replaced. God help us all if anyone tries.

During my ride with the PsyOp staff sergeant, he knew what I did because I lived in the Division area on Ardennes Street and the flash on my beret was from 2nd Battalion 505th Parachute Infantry Regiment, but I didn't know what he was talking about when he said he was "PsyOp." The adornment on his beret was from one of those "wimpy/pogue" units. "Pogue" was our slang term for those "other guys that aren't like us," or so we thought. At least that was what I thought at the time. I humored him for the ride and acted interested, but hey I needed the ride.

He told me about his deployments, and he had done a lot more than I had and had been to places I didn't even know we were in. Okay, so maybe I was wrong about the pogue thing. Then, he briefly told me about their mission, which was about influence, not finishing the enemy by means of fire and maneuver. At that time, I just figured it was simple and that bad guys needed to die but he told me about a humanitarian mission that prevented the strong hold of bad guys and how they saved lives.

Then the ride was over and that was the end of it. I went back to my cheap beer and dirty women. My original four-year tour of enlistment was over in 1994, little did I know that I would come back, a few more times. I left Division and got out of the Army but I still wanted to jump out of airplanes and shoot guns, it was like an addiction. I still wanted the cheap beer and dirty women but didn't have time for everything so . . . I chose jumping out of airplanes and got married.

I continued to shoot on a regular basis and even went through a police academy looking for something that resembled the military. I didn't become a cop but the academy was great for me.

As a civilian, I became a private investigator and a firearms instructor but I still wanted to jump out of airplanes and maybe even deploy. I went to a recruiter and tried to join the U.S. Army Reserves. There wasn't an Airborne infantry unit that deployed because they were all National Guard. However, he recommended a unit that did deploy and on jump status but I would have to learn Tactical PsyOp and no longer be an infantryman. I remembered the staff sergeant who gave me a ride that day several years before and agreed. That is how I got into the Tactical PsyOp game, and if they hadn't been an Airborne unit, I probably would have dropped the whole issue.

The unit was great and I was very impressed by the members of the unit. Several of them had been Special Forces, came from Ranger battalion, a couple of guys had been in Division, and there were even a few former Marines who I liked. I went through the PsyOp course and for the first time in the Army I really had to think and study hard to get through the instruction. It was intellectually challenging for me but I loved it. To my surprise it was fascinating and I was the field-phase Distinguished Graduate of the PsyOp Course.

At that time there were PsyOp teams that could stay deployed year round and get missions whenever, all we had to do was call Fort Bragg and have orders cut. It was a great time, but you can't be a civilian on Army pay, at least not a self-employed one.

I had another break in service, but after the September 11th terrorist attacks, I joined up again and was back at the unit training to deploy to Iraq. My entire first team that I started out with was in the same boat. We were all prior service that simply came back to serve and protect our families.

Things had changed while I was away; it wasn't as hard to get in the unit, and thank God because I couldn't have made it (I just wasn't a runner anymore, and a few too many hard landings had taken their toll on my back). So, being a little easier was fine by me; there were a lot of new troopers who didn't have any active-duty time, and that was the biggest change. That was never allowed before and I am still on the fence whether it is a good thing. I think leaders doing PsyOp in this environment should have active-duty time somewhere in their background to truly understand how to integrate or they should be officers . . . sorry, college don't count as a waiver here. In the past and for good reason generally, everyone had to have active-duty experience to get into the unit.

The PsyOp school seemed to be shorter, too, but they were doing great work. There were some good things that I felt were beneficial. Several of the guys had been to Afghanistan and had a lot of recent Warfighter experience. They were able to pass on great information to the guys getting ready to deploy to Iraq. If not for them, many of us would have gone in blind. The 7th PsyOp Group spent a lot of money getting schools and training that was the best I had seen in the Army, even in Division.

In Iraq when our TPT got to Sadr City, I noticed that the training and information simply missed some mission requirements that needed to be addressed. Training was training, but this was real and it was different. I thought, "fuck me running"; this was the most live-by-your-wits situation that I had ever been in. Keeping the heads of the team clear and completing this mission became the most important thing in life. There was an influence in Sadr City that controlled the people in such a way that was unlike what I had learned, and if not for my civilian experience and hobbies or thirty-three years of life experience and active-duty infantry experiences, I would not have known how to adjust to the environment.

Jaysh al Mehdi was the competing influence in Sadr City. There were no problems from Sunni Extremists or Zarqawi to deal with. This was a very real home-based insurgent militia trained by Hezbollah with the backing of Iran via the perverted Islam of Muqtada al Sadr. Officially, Jaysh al Mehdi wasn't considered to be a terrorist group or an insurgency, even though they are. I noticed that the cookie-cutter approach to Tactical PsyOp would not work in Sadr City.

The first issue was, all the products and messages that were available were designed to persuade against terrorism, and Jaysh al Mehdi is a terrorist group. However, the people's perception was that they were not, and perception is everything so it just didn't fit. The people considered them to be something other than terrorists. Even Jaysh al Mehdi spoke out against terrorism.

The products and messages provided to us ended up sounding like the same messages that Muqtada and Jaysh al Mehdi professed; we actually edified them, so that stopped quick. Our prepackaged messages and products actually gave Jaysh al Mehdi credibility, so we didn't use it.

Our TPT had to address the issues in Sadr City to determine what made Jaysh al Mehdi effective and understand their motivation. I couldn't ask the locals because initially I didn't know what buttons to push to get them to trust us or to open up. The best I could get was, "Everything is fine; it's God's will. Could you help me get my water fixed?" They told us that the terrorist always lived "someplace else."

However, we could see a different story from the type of murders and in the fear they had but they just could not talk about it.

If we were going to understand and find a way to influence the people in Sadr City and understand the controlling factors, we needed to go to the source and that meant Jaysh al Mehdi. This was somewhat off the Tactical PsyOp proverbial home page for most places in Iraq. Other places in Iraq had external forces that the people were afraid of and didn't have religious or cultural loyalties to their captors like they did in Sadr City.

The second major issue was that the products we had and the messages were geared towards Baghdad or Iraq, and that is typically fine. Sadr City was different here, too; again, perception is everything and the people of Sadr City didn't consider Sadr City to be the same as Baghdad. It was Sadr City, and Baghdad might as well have been on the other side of the planet for most of them. We needed to start from scratch. We needed our own PsyOp program separate from others.

To start we needed information from the controlling influence to be effective. It was not difficult to find Jaysh al Mehdi. Little did we know at the time that they were everywhere but we needed them vulnerable and off balance to really shake them down and find out how they justified what they did. If they were comfortable, they would just blend in and that wouldn't work. Just like with any bad guys, the likelihood of finding out much on their turf was slim. We needed them uncomfortable.

We couldn't do the traditional PsyOp technique of promoting a "key communicator" in the area and provide them with our message to promote. Key communicators were corrupted, and in order to create new key communicators that were not corrupt, we needed to determine everything about how to identify Jaysh al Mehdi that blended into the population by day to survey the people they covertly terrorized by night. We could find them at night when they were doing their illegal operations and using a blacked-out city to move freely around our patrols. That was the key. We needed to determine who was who, have the proper influence for each group, influence and write a PsyOp program for an infantry battalion to support a non-kinetic mission by doing PsyOp on their own.

There were quite a few good platoon sergeants and platoon leaders in the 3rd ID who wanted to be proactive. Many were willing to let us have as much rope as we needed to determine who was who in Sadr City. They hated Jaysh al Mehdi as much as we did and they were much like I was in Division. They wanted to find, fix, and finish the enemy by means of fire and maneuver. Well, being that I was an infantryman in the past, I understood their ways and could speak their language. I knew how they could scratch that itch. We couldn't necessarily "finish" the enemy but we could find them and fix them into a location (for a while, at least), and that is what we did.

We started hunting Jaysh al Mehdi and identifying them. Once we got a hold of them, they were more than happy to allow us to "study" them for a while, even if we didn't have enough on them to detain them or kill them in the process. Our TPT went on every mission we could that had to do with getting a hold of the bad guys; raids, cordon and search, and presence patrols were done at the right time and place so we could get our hands on Jaysh al Mehdi. The patrols were very restricted with what they could do, but talking and rattling the enemy's psychological cage was not a problem. Nor was it reported on because nobody thought it was a bad idea or wrong. That was helpful. I don't want to give away any techniques but before anybody goes ape shit; I rarely spoke to anyone for more than thirty minutes and nobody ever got hurt as part of the process. Given the right stimulus, people suck at hiding their emotions in any language. That's all I'm giving up on paper.

Jaysh al Mehdi, Punishment Committee Member. He was caught and almost shot the night of this photo for not wanting to show his hands. He was never officially detained. At this time we were not allowed to detain him even after he admitted to being Jaysh al Mehdi. Our own Military Commanders at the Brigade level tried to legitimize the same people that were killing the country, its people, and Americans.

Two of his buddies got away when they ditched a car down an alley and ran. Shooting them would have gotten us prison time. They were supposed to be legitimate but they still shot at us all the damn time whenever they thought they could get away with it. Commanders and Politics is a bad mix for Warfighters!

Oftentimes, we could get some Intel for the patrols while we were with them; they liked that, and it made our TPT an asset. That was the unspoken deal. We would help each other. Just like me being that young Division trooper not concerned with hearts and minds, we knew what 3rd ID wanted. We would get some Intel for them, and in return, we got face-to-face time with Jaysh al Mehdi. I could see and hear their rhetoric and got a sense of how they operated and controlled the people. And if we got a righteous opportunity to smack the shit out of a militia member, it was icing on the cake for what they did. These techniques are not in the PsyOp manual but they should be because it all worked.

We were able to create our own products and messages just for Sadr City to counter the Jaysh al Mehdi influence and grow our own key communicators because of what we did. With this knowledge, we were able to find the buttons to push when we talked to the people, were able to get them to trust us, and were able to get in their heads just enough to let them release their fear and replace it with some hope. This was the only way we could do our job and sell the concept of freedom.

Tactical PsyOp is only limited by creativity. Major events happen, Iraq has voted on major events while we do our job every day, and teaching the value of Democracy is a bitch. On one hand, we had the proactive ninth-grade civics lectures to motivate people to act, and on the other hand we had to promote them to not just act but act independently and fight Jaysh al Mehdi. It was especially difficult, when Jaysh al Mehdi is controlling so many people. The concentration of voters in Sadr City could actually make or break an election, so if we got caught slipping things were fucked. Sorry, but there just were not too many other ways to say it.

Things were a lot easier when the Army simply meant I could afford cheap beer and dirty women. I wanted to kill Muqtada, and we didn't have anything stopping us except opportunity and the creativity to facilitate it.

One night we got ambushed and Nacho did an excellent job getting us out of it. He drove his ass off to get us in the clear while in complete darkness under heavy fire. We had a grenade tossed in front of us and could have disabled us, leaving us in a world of shit, and Nacho was cool the whole time. There were easily a hundred Jaysh al Mehdi fighters shooting at our patrol.

The next day the Sadr City District Advisory Counsel wanted to have a sit-down because they said American forces killed some pregnant women during the firefight. I agree people were killed, I saw them get hit with a fifty-caliber machine gun, it was pretty bad and I doubt they lived, but these people died because they were shooting at the patrol. None were women.

The D.A.C. was heavily influenced by the Sadr Bureau, which is the "legitimate" side of Jaysh al Mehdi. That is some heated horseshit, because they were the same, only the name was different. Lieutenant Colonel Luck, the battalion commander, was asked to attend a meeting and he asked me to accompany him. This was a great opportunity to seize. The battalion commander was a great leader and he knew how to use us. Our job was to operate as his advisor and make him look good. We understood that if he looked good, everything would be fine because he was the face and voice of the American forces. The commander had to appear competent and strong; this was Iraq.

During the meeting, the Sadr Bureau attempted to leverage the situation and pin the commander down by telling us that Sadr City was safe and we were not needed there because we were too reckless. I was sitting next to the commander and as the Sadr Bureau spoke, I took notes and passed them to the commander, which he used as talking points to cut them off.

The commander was able to gain the angle of advantage. Not only did he leave them with no case, they were left open to more "occupation" because if the "wonderful" Jaysh al Mehdi was not shooting at us…then Sadr City was infiltrated by foreign fighters and we would be justified to stay longer with a greater force. Lieutenant Colonel Luck did a great job.

During the meeting, I recognized a man named Saed Kareem al Bukahti. I didn't think that he recognized me. He and I had run into each other a few times and at the time I didn't know that he was a negotiator for the Sadr Bureau. He was not a guy that I wanted a high profile with because he could shut people down from my contact.

Later, Saed Kareem and I ran into each other again. This time I was with a new commander and helping a different unit. That commander could have used some help. It was offered. Anyway, during the meeting with that commander, Saed Kareem stopped the meeting to stand up and greet me; the commander had to wait for us to get through all the common Iraqi meet-and-greet stuff. His question to me was, "Why didn't you say hello … after all this time, blah, blah." This was not a good situation; Saed Kareem knew me and he was ignoring the commander, I felt bad because that commander got punked by the entire Sadr Bureau.

I knew ahead of time all the players of the game and just couldn't get the opportunity to get heard. I don't want to make things worse so I won't use the commander's name but he was on all the wrong talking points. That was the day that everything changed. I watched a train wreck, back up, and do it again. The Sadr Bureau walked out of the meeting and a few days later was the bombing of the shrine in Summara. There was no American response and Jaysh al Medhi was slaughtering Sunnis in the street. I don't think Sunnis did that bombing. I think that Muqtada got the word about weakness in the area and took advantage of it.

PsyOp can go very far, we tend to operate autonomously. We can't win a war though ... we have no security element and a team is only three to four guys. It takes two guys to operate the guntruck on a patrol, one to drive and one to be a gunner. However, that is where creativity comes in. Here is a good example, after the Summara bombing we used our contacts that were still in Sadr City to report we had moved out to help a new unit but our contacts were still there and that is where the information came from.

Our supported battalion wouldn't listen so we took everything to the Tactical Human Intelligence Team (THT) sergeant. We always needed to find ways to get and share information in order to determine our effectiveness. If the supported unit won't help us then, most likely, they won't work with any of the attached units. That was the case and THT was happy to work with us. The THT sergeant pushed up the info from us as if his contacts had produced it, whoops, and no, I don't remember his name.

General Casey immediately put the entire country under a curfew and stopped the full-blown civil war. It's not uncommon for PsyOp and THT to work together in certain situations. It can be frowned upon by PsyOp command but sometimes shit just needs to be made to happen and anybody that says anything different never tried to stop genocide. The report that went to General Casey is shown later in the book.

That was a good piece of work and I am thankful to those THT guys. It was all about the creativity; that is what PsyOp today is all about. I acquired Saed Kareem's cell phone number from this guy that thought I could use it. Since Saed Kareem already knew about me and we weren't "working" Sadr City every day, it didn't matter if he knew me, and after the display he made . . . I couldn't ignore it.

He liked to think pretty highly of himself, so it was time to use that opportunity. A good PsyOp'er should be able to assess a person or group and immediately cater to it and make an encounter fit into his mission requirements and do it on the fly. I needed to see what he was thinking, thus finding out what Jaysh al Mehdi was pushing, and drop him some talking points to support our mission.

I used a female interpreter to call him on the phone and be flirtatious with him. It worked like a charm, he was like a giggly twelve-year-old boy with a boner and in an instant we had a straight connection to Muqtada al Sadr. We did this back and forth a few times and after about the third telephone meeting I asked him for a sit-down with Muqtada. He told me that we, he and I, had to ask Prime Minister Maliki first to make it happen and Maliki was a nice man so it would be okay.

It was a dead issue because nobody in the American Army would ever allow me, a lowly sergeant, to meet with Muqtada, getting a security detail to do the meeting would never get authorized. The team and I discussed it, this wasn't something I could order them to do. They came up with a plan, they were willing to put their asses on the line and sneak out of the wire (off the FOB) to make it happen. Nacho was convinced we could do it, Frank was all about doing our own stuff out of the wire, and Chesh was a voice of reason; it was pretty surreal. This event was so important that they were willing to be captured on an unsanctioned mission that could probably end in having their heads cut off. We KNEW what Jaysh al Mehdi was capable of but we hated them.

My mission would be to make Saed Kareem and Muqtada "think" that we were so important that we shouldn't be fucked with. We needed a security guarantee and enough sack to make it all happen, that part we could do. The unforeseen factors were, if we did make it back alive, we couldn't follow through on anything because it wouldn't stay quiet; we couldn't accomplish anything at that level alone and we would have to worry about going to a military prison. That is where it stopped, I pussed out. Ain't that a bitch!

However, the fact that Saed Kareem told me the quasi-chain of command between Maliki and Muqtada was interesting. Basically, the prime minister was the first link below Muqtada. The man who is running the country, the prime minister, an elected official, set appointments for Muqtada. Why wouldn't I be able to go straight to Muqtada? . . . an interesting future for Iraq.

Empowerment Is The Key

Chapter 7

If you are wondering what a typical patrol in Sadr City is like, I have illustrated information from a few different patrols. Some factors were a constant, regardless of the patrol. A lot of good people were always afraid because Jaysh al Mehdi was around in some way, and things could go from typical to extraordinary very fast.

The information that you read is factually accurate; however, the specific data about our techniques have been removed or altered for operational security and Intel reasons. A lot more went on than you see here, but this is what a typical Situation Report (Sitrep) might look like. I even left in the grammar errors for realism. Sitreps have to be sent to higher-ups every day, and then they should be read and analyzed to refine operations. These are things we reported on and they actually happened.

The accusations and references to Muqtada and Jaysh al Mehdi are real. Analyze the contradictions regarding the Iraqi Police for yourself.

Excerpts:

Tactical PsyOp Team (TPT) 1412: Accompany 3rd Battalion 15th Infantry Regiment, 3rd Infantry Division Presence Patrol in Sadr City, Iraq:

The patrol's first stop was at the *** Iraqi Police station. PsyOp Team Sergeant spoke with a Lt. Col. at the station and inquired as to who has authority to carry weapons in Sadr City. The Lt. Col. stated that only Coalition Forces, Iraqi Army (IA), and Iraqi Police are authorized to carry weapons, but not Jaysh al Mehdi. The Lt. Col. also stated that if Jaysh al Mehdi is found carrying weapons without a permit, that Coalition Forces could call his Iraqi Police station and that they would arrest any Jaysh al Mehdi members who are carrying illegal weapons. The PsyOp Team Sergeant then asked if the Lt. Col. was aware that other Iraqi Police stations in Sadr City were under the control of the Jaysh al Mehdi, and he said that some were but he wasn't sure which ones. The PsyOp Team Sergeant asked if his station was under Jaysh al Mehdi control. The Lt. Col. advised that it was not under Jaysh al Mehdi control.

After speaking with the Lt. Col., the PsyOp Team Sergeant spoke with several prisoners in the jail. The PsyOp Team Sergeant attempted to influence attitudes by spending several minutes discussing crimes committed by Anti-Iraqi Forces (AIF). During the conversation with the prisoners, the PsyOp Team Sergeant told them that they lived in a Democracy and had a right to speak out against crime. The prisoners unanimously claimed that Jaysh al Mehdi committed these crimes. Two prisoners asked to speak with the PsyOp Team Sergeant in private, and the PsyOp Team Sergeant did so with the Patrol Leader. The first prisoner named *** was in prison for allegedly murdering a Jaysh al Mehdi member. *** stated that he was a [Occupation Deleted] and the real reason for his imprisonment was that during a job, he realized that he was at a Jaysh al Mehdi Punishment Committee member's house, and he became visibly nervous. The people at the house noticed that he became suspicious, felt he could identify them or make trouble, so he was arrested for murder.

Another prisoner named *** stated that he was in prison for murdering a high-ranking Jaysh al Mehdi member. He did not deny that he committed the crime. The Jaysh al Mehdi member that was murdered was second in command under ***. He stated that the reason he murdered the Jaysh al Mehdi member was to avenge his brother's murder by the Jaysh al Mehdi because their sister worked at the Ministry of Interior and was threatened if she did not quit. So her brother tried to defend his sister and was killed by Jaysh al Mehdi. *** stated that he also had another brother that is willing to infiltrate the Jaysh al Mehdi to collect Intel on their criminal activity. The PsyOp Team Sergeant provided *** with his cell number and *** said he would give it to his brother when he saw him.

Tactical PsyOp Team (TPT) 1412: Accompany 2nd Battalion 22nd Infantry Regiment, 10th Mountain Division Presence Patrol in Sadr City, Iraq:

The patrol stopped in vicinity of *** in the commercial area of ***. Several people were spoken to by the patrol as the patrol walked through the area and passed out literature. Many people responded favorably. However, there was a group of six Local Nationals (LNs) that tore up the literature and threw it on the ground in front of the patrol. From that point, people became fearful of accepting the literature from the members of the patrol. The PsyOp Team Sergeant coached the Platoon Leader on how to speak with the Local Nationals regarding certain information topics with talking points.

A man named *** approached the PsyOp Team Sergeant discreetly and asked for another phone number to contact Coalition Forces directly because the phone number on the literature is a Ministry of Interior number, and he felt that the Ministry of Interior could not be trusted. *** provided the PsyOp Team Sergeant with his phone number: *** for later contact.

Tactical PsyOp Team (TPT) 1412: Accompany 3rd Battalion 15th Infantry Regiment, 3rd Infantry Division Presence Patrol in Sadr City, Iraq:

During the patrol, a Local National, later identified as ***, was stopped in the vicinity of ***. He was working as a guard and was in possession of one AK-47 and a chest rig full of AK magazines. Several men that sat near him, as he slept on a grassy center island of the street, ran from the area and headed down an alley at the same time the patrol stopped. The Patrol Leader used *** to call out to the men in the alleyway as a ruse in order to bring them to us, so that the patrol would not be potentially ambushed. The men refused to comply. It appeared that they were hiding from the patrol and possibly protecting something. The patrol made several attempts to make contact with the men peacefully, but they still refused to comply. Finally, the PsyOp Team Sergeant and the patrol went after them, but they could not be found. Because of his fear of being arrested for breaking the law, *** then told the PsyOp Team Sergeant of a nearby location of a man named ***. He stated that *** is a high ranking Jaysh al Mehdi member that was potentially hiding weapons, and that maybe the men that ran from the patrol did so to warn him. The Patrol Leader and the PsyOp Team Sergeant discussed the situation and were familiar with the name *** gave.

The patrol and the PsyOp Team Sergeant made entry and searched the home to look for the Jaysh al Mehdi leader. The home was on the same alley where the men ran. Three women and three of *** sons were at the home but *** was not there. At the request of the Platoon Leader, the PsyOp Team Sergeant spoke with two of the sons separately; both had conflicting stories as to the present location of their father. One son stated that his father was at a funeral for their cousin and left by bus that morning. The other son stated that his father was on a three-day business trip and left with their uncle yesterday. The oldest son, ***, possessed an Iraqi Police ID card. While in the home, the phone rang, and the PsyOp Team Sergeant told the Platoon Leader's interpreter to answer the call. The caller was the man we were looking for and he believed the interpreter was his wife. The interpreter stated that the caller sounded out of breath when he stated that he "made it" to the Sadr Bureau. He then instructed his family not to open the door because Americans were outside.

During the search of the home, the PsyOp Team Sergeant identified pages of Census information regarding addresses and names of people within Sadr City. The information indicated names and ages of occupants of individual residences. Co-located in the same stack of information were partially blank sheets from the "Million-Person Petition" that was used by Jaysh al Mehdi in an attempt to have Coalition Forces removed from Sadr City. It appeared that names might have been fraudulently transcribed from the Census information to the petition. The PsyOp Team Sergeant asked the youngest son where his father got the Census information. The son informed the PsyOp Team Sergeant that the Mayor had provided the information to his father. Some other items of interest included an SKS rifle and a Glock 9 mm pistol. The eldest son possessed a legitimate-looking Iraqi Police ID card and stated that the Glock pistol belonged to him. Iraqi Police Officers carry Glock pistols.

A second phone call from *** was made to the home, and again, the interpreter answered the phone. This time, *** requested to speak with one of his sons. The youngest son was given guidance to tell his father that it was safe to come home, but during the phone conversation, the son never advised his father it was safe to return, and *** did not return while we were there.

The guard *** provided the following information during a casual conversation with the PsyOp Team Sergeant: He was once an Iraqi Police Officer and showed us his old Police ID card to prove it, but he had to quit because he was being coerced by the Jaysh al Mehdi and was afraid of being killed. Currently, *** works as a guard and makes little money to support his family. He was very susceptible to PsyOp themes and talking points because of the problems created by Jaysh al Mehdi, and he does not believe Jaysh al Mehdi or Muqtada al Sadr are good for Iraq. He feels they are becoming worse than Saddam Hussein was.

During a conversation where the PsyOp Team Sergeant spoke about PsyOp themes and talking points, the guard, ***, felt empowered and wanted to help. He provided the PsyOp Team Sergeant with very specific information regarding events that the PsyOp Team Sergeant had personal knowledge of, amongst other things, the murder of two women that were found tortured with notes claiming that they had collaborated with U.S. Forces. Again, the info *** gave was very accurate to the best of the PsyOp Team Sergeant's knowledge and he provided a sense of sincerity in his actions as he spoke. He also spoke accurately of a man by the "nickname" or "code name" of *** that was posing as an Iraqi Police Officer. He had fake Iraqi Police

ID cards and used fake Iraqi Police trucks to commit assassinations. The info previously learned regarding the murders of the females is listed in the PsyOp Sitrep dated *** and the info regarding code name *** is listed in the PsyOp Sitrep dated ***.

These consistencies make the rest of his statements seem very credible. The following is additional info provided by *** regarding Jaysh al Mehdi activities and members, some of which are high ranking:

- Name *** / Sector *** / Phone number ***

    Has close and direct contact with Muqtada al Sadr. *** meets with Sheik *** at the *** Mosque, on a daily basis between 2030–2100 hrs, in Sector ***. They discuss ways to kill Americans. Lately, they have been discussing killing Americans when they dismount to conduct an arrest. Sheik *** is known for killing Iraqi Army soldiers and then using their vehicles to conduct Jaysh al Mehdi operations. Sheik *** lives in the mosque where they meet.

- Name *** according to PsyOp Sitrep dated: *** / Sector *** / Phone Number ***

    *** has a fake Iraqi Police truck, assassinates people, and after taking them to an undisclosed location on a street known locally as *** (according to Col. *** of the *** Iraqi Police Station), five newly built houses near *** have very suspicious occupants; PsyOp Sitrep dated ***. He is believed to kidnap people when they are at the *** Market.

- Name *** / 2 possible phone numbers: *** or ***

  *** is a bodyguard for the Minister of Health and a Jaysh al Mehdi member. The guard that gave this information has witnessed *** firing RPGs at American armored vehicles during last year's Sadr City uprising.

- Name *** / Sector *** / Phone number ***

  *** is a weapons dealer for the Jaysh al Mehdi.

- Name *** (aka ***) / Sector ***

  *** drives a white Toyota ***. He is the assistant to ***, and is a friend of Muqtada al Sadr and hates Sustani very much. He spends most of his time with *** in Sector ***.

- Name *** / Sector ***

  *** took the place of ***, who was killed by the Americans during last year's Sadr City uprising. *** has not been seen in several months. *** is known to coordinate tortures at a school in Sector ***. According to the guard, *** ordered the method of torture, and the murder of the two women. PsyOp Sitrep dated ***. He stated that the reasoning behind the murders was to keep people from talking with the Americans and to make the Americans look bad. The guard had unassisted knowledge of the notes found on the bodies, including what was written on the notes and the location of the notes on the bodies.

Using PsyOp themes and talking points is very effective when establishing rapport and evaluating people's susceptibilities. While talking to ***, he felt empowered by the PsyOp Team Sergeant, and as a result, he offered to help his country. The potential informant, ***, is willing to contact the S-2 interpreter on Sundays and Thursdays between 0900–1200 hrs and update Coalition Forces with any information he finds out. He is willing to come to the FOB and positively identify locations of all the people listed above.

Tactical PsyOp Team (TPT) 1412: Accompany 2nd Battalion 22nd Infantry Regiment, 10th Mountain Division Presence Patrol in Sadr City, Iraq:

The patrol dismounted in Sector *** and the Patrol Leader spoke with Local Nationals at a generator station. During the conversation, the PsyOp Team Sergeant coached the Patrol Leader on what to say. The Local Nationals stated that the Jaysh al Mehdi patrols the area often and there are a lot of people killed locally. Though the Local Nationals did not say specifically that the Jaysh al Mehdi was responsible, he alluded to it several times. The Local Nationals would nod their heads to confirm Jaysh al Mehdi, but when asked specifically, they seemed too afraid to say the name out loud. The Patrol Leader attempted to instill a sense of empowerment by telling the man that he was very brave to talk about issues because others are afraid to, and that murder/kidnapping are illegal and wrong. The Local Nationals agreed and stated that he would always remember this conversation in the future, when he spoke to his friends or family. The Local National seemed to absorb the concepts of the conversation and was given a Tips Line Key Chain.

The patrol was called to assist the 1st Platoon and waited in the vicinity of ***. Then the patrol moved to *** and the PsyOp Team

Sergeant spoke to three Local Nationals while the Patrol Leader received info on the radio. The conversation was cut short and the men were given Tip Line Key Chains.

The patrol was deployed to assist two other platoons that were in a firefight. The patrol responded and was en route to the link-up to assist. Then our patrol was in a sustained firefight for approximately 20 minutes and was shot at from both sides of the street in the city that was completely blacked out. Approximately 100 enemy personnel fired from rooftops and from alleyways. The PsyOp Team Sergeant observed approximately 7–10 men (not just their muzzle flashes) shooting with AK-47s and an RPK within 25 meters of our vehicle, as we drove by on our way to reinforce another platoon. The PsyOp Team Sergeant observed his gunner behind us kill a man with an RPK as he turned to shoot us. Tracers streaked across our front as we drove. Several gunners on the patrol returned fire while being shot at. An explosive device was detonated as the patrol passed it and it exploded just in front of the Tactical PsyOp Team vehicle. The PsyOp Assistant Team Sergeant was in the driver position and observed muzzle flash at eye level several times within 25 meters.

The ambush lasted from the corner of *** and *** as we traveled North to the corner of *** and *** and we turned West to the corner of *** and ***, and then as we traveled South to the corner of *** and *** back *** to the original corner of *** and ***. The entire trip spanned across seven sectors North then seven sectors back. The platoon we were attempting to reinforce broke contact prior to our link-up.

PSYOP TEAM SERGEANT'S ASSESSMENT:

The Jaysh al Mehdi appears to be getting bolder and bolder. The PsyOp Team Sergeant believes there are several reasons for this, one of which is a lack of lethal response to these Jaysh al Mehdi crimes. The supported unit has received increased direct fire attacks lately, while we are on patrol with them, and it as been reported that the Jaysh al Mehdi has taken a hard line response to raids and the appearance of raids. This is believed to be done to keep their people from being detained. The PsyOp Team Sergeant believes that they are acting with an above-the-law mentality and as if they are the only legitimate force in Sadr City.

The people of Sadr City have recently been more vocal about their dislike for the Jaysh al Mehdi but are still very afraid of them because of corruption at the Ministry of Interior and with local Iraqi Police. The Jaysh al Mehdi appears to be untouchable. The PsyOp Team Sergeant believes that the people of Sadr City truly believe that the only honest forces that can save them from the Jaysh al Mehdi are Coalition Forces. Thus, the Jaysh al Mehdi is attempting to show dominance towards Coalition Forces so they can continue to control the people by fear.

Tactical PsyOp Team (TPT) 1412: Accompany 2nd Battalion 22nd Infantry Regiment, 10th Mountain Division Presence Patrol in Sadr City, Iraq:

PRIOR RELEVANT INFORMATION:

In the vicinity of ***, the patrol stopped at a music store on Route *** because we observed a TV playing a video that depicted Jaysh al Mehdi members dressed all in black and carrying weapons. The PsyOp Team Sergeant spoke to the Patrol Leader and confirmed an earlier Intel report about an ice cream parlor that was on Route *** that had been a possible Jaysh al Mehdi hang-out where weapons were sold. The music store that was playing the video just happened to be next door to an ice cream parlor on Route ***. With this information, the Patrol Leader and the PsyOp Team Sergeant were very cautious about contacting the music store employees and collecting the Jaysh al Mehdi Propaganda video disc because it was next door to an area that we believed sold weapons for the Jaysh al Mehdi..

The PsyOp Team Sergeant made contact with the music store employee as the patrol provided security. There were approximately forty military-age men standing outside the store watching the video of Jaysh al Mehdi members dancing around on a street near a large poster of Muqtada al Sadr that was displayed on the hood of a car. The Jaysh al Mehdi members in the video all carried weapons as they danced. The crowd at the video store seemed to get very tense as the patrol approached. The PsyOp Team Sergeant decided to prioritize getting the video rather than making a big attempt at conducting a face-to-face engagement with the crowd because they already appeared upset, and the actual music shop owner had "disappeared" before we made contact. The PsyOp Team Sergeant did not want to take a chance at a confrontation or getting distracted, and lose the opportunity to seize the video.

One young boy, approximately twelve years old, was at the music shop and appeared to be somewhat disoriented as to where things were, as if he didn't actually work there. The PsyOp Team Sergeant stated in a very nice way that he liked the music on the video and wanted to purchase a copy. The young boy seemed nervous and stated that he did not know where a copy of the video was. The PsyOp Team Sergeant convinced him that he really needed a copy and the boy picked a random disc on a table and tried to give it to the PsyOp Team Sergeant. Meanwhile, the crowd outside was becoming more agitated. It appeared that the boy was trying to prevent the PsyOp

Team Sergeant from getting the video. The PsyOp Team Sergeant told the boy that he wanted the one out of the video machine. The PsyOp Team Sergeant gave the boy $20 for the video disc as the crowd began to gather and grow outside, probably from the ice cream parlor, and things were getting very tense. The PsyOp Team Sergeant and the Patrol Leader agreed that the patrol should leave immediately because of the tense situation, and we already had a copy of the video disc.

While the PsyOp Team Sergeant and Patrol Leader were discussing what to do, we had to wait a minute because the boy asked to quickly speak to the PsyOp Team Sergeant's interpreter. The boy was adamant about letting him know that the video showed Jaysh al Mehdi "protecting" people as they visited a shrine in Karbalah earlier in September. The patrol departed the area. The people became more vocally angry and began to chant.

Contents of the Video: PSYOP TEAM SERGEANT'S ASSESSMENT

The video has several messages that the producer appears to have purposely put on the finished product for a specific reason. The video was well produced and may be a call to arms by the Jaysh al Mehdi for Muqtada, as well as the opposite. It appears that the Jaysh al Mehdi feels they were victorious during the uprising in Najaf and they have God on their side, so they want Muqtada al Sadr to do the same again. All the men in the video openly carried Sadr Bureau ID badges. The music lyrics on the video are very violent and it ends with the words, "Show them Hell."

Contents of the Video: PSYOP TEAM SERGEANT'S REPORT OF PROPAGANDA

The video is of Jaysh al Mehdi members making several statements inciting and encouraging violence against the "Americans." They are all carrying weapons. The video also displays a sniper rifle with a scope, several RPKs, and an RPG. These depictions appear to be recent and there was an older clip that was edited from the uprising that showed a man shooting a belt-fed crew serve weapon. During the video, Iraqi Police and Iraqi Army soldiers from Sadr City were seen passing the group of Jaysh al Mehdi members that were carrying weapons illegally. The Iraqi Army and the Iraqi Police appeared to allow them to carry and display their weapons without consequence. The demonstration was notably in Sadr City with easily identifiable landmarks, as the Iraqi Security Forces did nothing to enforce the law and stop Jaysh al Mehdi from carrying weapons.

At the time in the video (17SEP05 and 18SEP05 shown during the video), Jaysh al Mehdi members were seen by the Iraqi Police while they were in Sadr City near the power station on Route ***. The number seen on the side of the Iraqi Police truck is 2535 and the Iraqi Army truck was a green dual-cab truck with a primer-colored square on the rear driver-side door. Neither one of these Iraqi Security Forces groups did anything to stop the men that were illegally carrying weapons openly on a Sadr City street. During the video, the cameraman filmed an ID badge and the ID badge was from the Sadr Bureau. All of the men wore the same badge. They all refer to Muqtada al Sadr as "Saed."

The following is a list of the translated verbal messages heard on the video; the messages were stated by the Jaysh al Mehdi members:

- He deserves our sacrifices for him.
- The Saed will protect it (the Jaysh al Mehdi).
- Sadr never sleeps.
- Sadr is like our father and we ask God to keep him safe.
- God has sent Muqtada, and because of him, Israel and America know him very well.
- Alawi is nothing compared to Muqtada.
- This is the last time we want Alawi.
- We will be like artillery to destroy Alawi.
- If you don't like the Jaysh al Mehdi then go fuck yourselves (paraphrased).
- When Muqtada carries the RPG, then everything is okay.
- Referring to the battle in Najaf, the Mayor of Najaf and the Minister of Defense are both sons of bitches. The old Baathist (Alawi) even said if the Shrine (in Najaf) is destroyed, I don't care. Muqtada called for his army to destroy them all ... and you know how many planes were destroyed in Najaf. The Right was beside them, and the Imam Mehdi appeared to them.
- We promised our leader to stay loyal soldiers and were ready to sacrifice for great Iraq.

Another portion of the video was shot from a place in the town of Lateefia and men wore body armor worn by Iraqi Police. A possible doctor with a stethoscope and men in the usual Jaysh al Mehdi canary-yellow shirts, an RPG, and a sniper rifle were seen. There were still several men seen in the usual black Jaysh al Mehdi attire.

The following are excerpts from the music that played on the video:

- They (Americans) would confront him (Muqtada al Sadr) if they were strong.
- The enemy (Americans) are scared.
- Bush and his followers are scared of us.
- One of us is equal to 100 of the Americans.
- We are ready to sacrifice our souls for Sadr. He tired them out. We promised that we would stay with you for all time. Muqtada, you are our everything.

There was one point in the video when the cameramen were talking and one of them asked, "Where is your shop?" The other man then answered "In sector *** in Merhedi" (located in Sadr City).

The following are more lyrical excerpts:

- Anybody who follows you has everything.
- Muqtada, you are like a treasure to our country.
- We honor you, we are ready to sacrifice.
- We will never stop until the end.
- You are the greatest lesson to us and we promise you again.
- You are like a lion.
- Muqtada is the best son; he is just like his father.

A truck with a machine gun on it drove by and played a loudspeaker broadcast that stated the following: "The Saed gave us the order and we protect it." Behind the truck was a red fire truck with a large Muqtada poster attached to it.

The following are more lyrical excerpts:

- His thoughts and the way he acts is like the Imam Abbas and his voice is heard in every city.
- He never fears.

- When the enemy sees him they flee. We are supported by the Imam.
- We are the men of the city and we promise you.
- You are the son of Sadr and you are the Lion.
- Muqtada . . . make them afraid and defeat the armies.
- We are your support and we stay with you to the last blood.
- Do whatever you can to remind them of your father.
- Go do whatever you want, we are your soldiers.
- You are supported by Imam Ali.
- Make them afraid.
- Show them Hell.

We Kept Our Promise
Chapter 8

I'm not a "black helicopter" conspiracy theorist guy; however, sometimes I wonder. This chapter is inspired by the events of an email thread sent from my supported unit's higher command (not meant for me to see) and an argument I had with my command. We were sending Sitreps day after day about the events going on. In return, I was threatened with being relieved in Sadr City . That was a kick in the sack.

Our supported unit's higher command didn't like the reports I sent; the more I sent, the more he didn't like it. The Iraqi Police jails were a great place to find information about Jaysh al Mehdi for the supported unit and spread our messages. The supported unit's higher command didn't like me going to the jails and asking questions. Thus, my command at the lower level started pulling on me to draw more distinct lines between Intel and PsyOp, then pushing me to stay on the PsyOp side only. Those two things simply go hand-in-hand. How can I determine what to do or what is working if I don't ask questions?

When Intel came to me during these engagements it was an impact indicator of the trust that was established. If there was no

Intel, more than likely the trust was not well established and rapport was weak. The command wanted a one-way information operation. That was not my job nor was it effective. We had to influence attitudes to change behavior that supports the U.S. National Objective.

Other soldiers just could not get Intel and I could. I was there and it actually helped me to do it myself . . . PsyOp is two-way Intel. First, we get information to establish who we are talking to and determine their motivation. Based on our quick initial Intel as a Psyop'er we effectively use disinformation to counter them one way or use proactive talking points to motivate their actions towards our objective. None of this can be done without the initial assessment of the group or person. In Iraq, rapport was most easily established by allowing good people that were afraid the opportunity to vent their emotions. Thus, out came the Intel. I didn't do anything with Intel except pass it up the chain. Why didn't he want it?

My biggest mistake was being honest about it. We left home, left our kids, to go to Iraq and do good. Maybe they didn't want to deal with some of the madness.

So I was sent for a psych eval, to determine if I had a fascination with death and why I was "controlling assets" ("assets" are what the Army calls informants) because of the info I sent them. I didn't make the dead people, I just reported how they died, who killed them, and the circumstances regarding the situation. They were not "assets" being controlled by me. Some were actually brave people, who volunteered to provide atmospheric information about what was happening so we could measure our effectiveness. The fact that they were even willing to stay in touch without being paid meant that we were more effective; they would have been killed if found out. They trusted us and we had a responsibility to keep our promises.

By the way, the psych eval led to nothing except for the shrink wanting me to get him out of the wire on a patrol with my team. That's when the reprimand came. I got a warning with the "threat" of being relieved if I didn't start doing things another way. They actually doubted the "whispered truth" we reported on in Sadr Ciy and the work we had done because the supported unit's higher command hadn't seen it for himself.

As a result of my . . . let's just call it a new "probation" . . . my team was restructured and Chesh came on board. He was the same rank as me so that was an easy move for my command. If I were relieved Chesh would take over. That was a good idea; however, even though I had never worked with Chesh I knew he was an honest man and I banked on him.

That email thread I referred to from the supported unit's higher command looked something like this and I will never forget the words: It said, "I know the Mehdi Militia are not a bunch of choir boys but I have yet to see them standing next to any dead bodies." The man that wrote that was a full bird colonel that NEVER patrolled the city. Okay, that wasn't his job. Fine, then listen to the information from people that do patrol Sadr City. I felt like I was in a bad war action movie asking, "Do we get to win this time?"

No problem, it was time to put up or shut up. I had to make some money and get paid or die trying for my work. That meant if I was worth my salt I needed to get video of the "whispered truth." I had to get a visual aid for the slower kids in the class (don't judge me; I was the slow kid and can say that).

I couldn't figure out how to get people to speak outside of a whisper at night and now I needed a voluntarily willing participant during the day, on video. Aint't that a bitch!

The video wasn't the primary mission. It was on order as the opportunity could be produced because we still had to stay focused on what was really important; I couldn't be distracted with that nonsense. I just threw some bullshit in my reports to keep my command off of my back while the team and I worked. It wasn't a lie, it was just a savvy version of the truth. Chesh was a great help with the reports, an excellent choice to succeed me. The supported unit received a separate report, not so savvy, to continue the operations we were doing. It wasn't their fault that they had a "see no evil" higher command.

Routinely, we worked the jails by visiting once or twice a week on a patrol to see who was there while the patrol leader spoke to an Iraqi Police commander. Many people in the jails were put there wrongly for having a beef with Jaysh al Mehdi. Others were there because there is no arraignment or bond system; Iraq doesn't have an innocent until proven guilty concept like America does. I don't expect this to make any sense at first. From the outside, I wouldn't buy it for a dollar either because we think of our jails in America as a place for criminals. Things are different in Iraq because many innocent people are held in jail.

One night at the Hababiya Iraqi Police Station, I was assessing what people were there for. Murder this, mistake that, I don't have a passport, whatever, same old shit. Then we addressed the group with our talking points and that is when the eyes lit up. It's a captive audience, use it. As logic would have it Jaysh al Mehdi wouldn't be spending any time in a Sadr City jail, they didn't go to jail. Jail was for people that weren't Jaysh al Mehdi.

During the engagement a man raised his hand and asked to speak to us. That took balls, usually we had to identify people to pull into a side room and make it look like they didn't want to go for them to feel safe. Then they would spill their guts to us. This guy volunteered in the open. Let's call him Mr. Ed so I keep it clear.

We pulled Mr. Ed into a room and he told us that he had information about IEDs Jaysh al Mehdi had. I wasn't going to have my chain yanked so I asked for more. He actually had the info and that is all I can say. I asked him why he was there and he told me that he and his uncle were waiting for release but the family couldn't afford the bribe to get them out. Mr. Ed was valuable and what PsyOp calls susceptible; otherwise, he wouldn't have spoke up with this kind of info. He truly wanted a better Iraq.

The platoon sergeant and I spoke about it. We had to get Mr. Ed and his uncle out. We agreed to take them to the FOB and debrief them. But we needed to get them out without raising suspicion. I asked the Iraqi Police commander why this man was here and he told me that he was being processed out ... holy shit, that meant Mr. Ed told me the truth again. So I lied and threw a raging, kicking, screaming fit worthy of an Academy Award. I told the IPs that they were harboring known terrorists that killed Americans and since we were not told every one of them was going to jail.

I told them that I was taking them with me, he wanted me to sign their sign-out log. I told them ... you know who the fuck I am, you sign it; then we all left holding our breath. Good thing there wasn't an officer on that patrol.

We got them back to the FOB Hope and the THT spoke to them. I wrote up a report and went to bed. The Intel Officer, THT, and I agreed to hold onto these guys because we couldn't take them back to the IP station now, they would end up dead for fear of talking to us. I intended to talk to Mr. Ed and his uncle when I woke up but somebody sent them back to the IP station while I was sleeping. Somehow, it was a communication error. My heart sank.

The patrol we were with was Delta Company so I went to their commander and asked if they could be picked up. He was a very proactive man so I had confidence he would help. He said that he couldn't "just pick them up" but the patrol that was out of the wire would check on them. Shit, I didn't want to get these guys killed and I knew it was coming.

They were there two more days. Then when a patrol went out to check on Mr. Ed and his uncle, the IPs told the patrol leader that the only reason these men were held was because the Delta Company commander had asked for them to be held. Whoops, that was what we call a target of opportunity. I talked to the Delta Company commander and it was "game on." He put his ass on the line for us to pick up Mr. Ed and his uncle. And I heard there was a report at the same station of an IED being stored there.

We went to the IP Station in Hababiya and got Mr. Ed and his uncle for the second time. Unfortunately, the door where the files were was locked and nobody had the key. We needed that door open to get their passports and anything that identified them. A nice American soldier blew the door off the hinges while looking for that IED and we were able to get the passports.

We released Mr. Ed and his uncle that night and gave them money to get to the FOB the next day. The next day they both showed up with man-kisses for everyone, I never got into the man-kiss thing but I am a PsyOp'er. If they want to kiss, I kiss but that is as far as it goes without a shave and some falafel.

Mr. Ed's uncle was too afraid to talk, so he thanked me and left. Mr. Ed wanted to talk and I just gave him a venue. He showed me the scars of his torture during the interview and told me how Jaysh al Mehdi had murdered eight people at the Major Crimes unit, three from the Hababiya IP Station. He told me his story about the whispered truth for about forty-five minutes. He gave the same verbal picture as the rest of the people. Rape, murder, torture, kidnapping, corrupt officials, and Muqtada.

The Iraqi Ministry of Defense, Ministry of Interior, and my supported unit's higher command threw a shit fit. Then came what was called a DD Form 15-6 investigation over the entire thing. Everybody involved had to deal with that.

Mr. Ed left Sadr City to start over again. He returned out of the blue one day, on his own, and asked me what I wanted of him. In PsyOp, that is what we call a positive Impact Indicator. I told him, only his friendship, he was a free man and nobody owned him. He cried and I never saw him again. That was my opportunity to model to him how he should be treated.

I believe in this mission and I believe in freedom for all. I left my kids at home alone to be here and they're not going to fight a war that Daddy should have taken care of. Doing this one act of getting him and his uncle out of that jail affected many people. It affected the two of them because they are alive and whispering the story of how Americans were willing to blow doors off of hinges to free them. All because they took a chance and spoke up like free men.

They went outside of the learned helplessness mode and it freed them. Also, the thirty to forty other men in that jail observed the same thing. They all saw how acting independently was rewarded with a positive action. If only ten percent of those people receive that message and permeate it to their tribe and family—we win a little in the Arab world and the Middle East. This is another example of something not in the PsyOp handbook but should be.

The interview that Mr. Ed gave me was willingly and voluntarily videotaped on the anniversary of the terrorist attacks in New York City, September 11. God does work in amazing ways, not even I can ignore this one. Mr. Ed even pulled his shirt off to show his scars and what torture does to a human body. A lot of trust came from a man who lives in a culture that felt scorned by the scandal at Abu Ghraib Prison.

I still have a copy of the video and I gave it to that commander who wrote how he "had yet to see the Mehdi Militia standing next to any dead bodies." Nothing became of that DD Form 15-6 investigation; maybe because I turned in a copy of the video with my statement.

The murders and torture committed at the Hababiya IP station and the Major Crimes unit in Adhamiya were never investigated and I am sure it continued.

Weapons of Mass Destruction WMD

Chapter 9

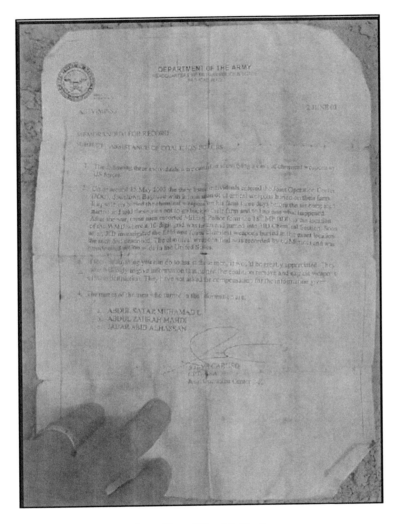

Contributed By: M. Parker

Next is the typed version (with some needed grammar corrections) of the letter that has been photographed above, to make it easier for you to read. I believe that it will surprise you. I personally have not seen the "60 Minutes" episode referred to in the letter.

DEPARTMENT OF THE ARMY

HEADQUARTERS, 18ᵀᴴ MILITARY POLICE BRIGADE

BAGHDAD, IRAQ

AETV-MP-S3 2JUN03

MEMORANDUM OF RECORD

SUBJECT: ASSISTANCE OF COALITION FORCES

1. The following individuals were crucial in identifying a cache of Chemical Weapons to U.S. Forces.

2. On or Around 15 May 2003, the three individuals listed entered the Joint Operations Center (JOC), downtown Baghdad with information of Chemical Weapons buried on their farm. An Iraqi Soldier buried the Chemical Weapons on his farm three days before the Air Campaign started and told these men to go back to their farm and tell no one what happened. After the War, these men escorted Military Police from the 18th MP Brigade (BDE) to the location of the WMD where a 10-digit grid was taken and turned into the 3rd Infantry Division (3ID) Chemical Section. Soon after, the 3rd Infantry Division (3ID) investigated the field and found Chemical Weapons buried in the same exact location the men had described. The Chemical Weapons find was recorded by "60 Minutes" and was broadcast nationwide in the United States.

3. If there is anything you can do to assist these men, it would be greatly appreciated. They came willingly to give

information that helped the Coalition remove and exploit weapons of mass destruction. They have not asked for compensation for the information given.

4. The names of the men that turned in the information are:

(I have deleted their names to help keep them protected.)

The letter was signed by an officer working at the Joint Operations Center and I don't want to dime him out because military officers can get reprimanded for stupid things like . . . trying to help others. For some reason, after officers reach a certain level in their career, people seem to not matter as much.

Prior to the liberation of Iraq, the Bush administration made a good argument for the invasion. One of the biggest reasons was Saddam's capability of producing weapons of mass destruction. America had just been hit by a reasonably low-tech yet high-concept-type attack carried out at the World Trade Center in New York City. We were vulnerable, angry, and scared. No doubt Saddam was a bad man, simply put, but did he have the capability to produce weapons of mass destruction like our government claimed? Yes, he did have the capability because we have evidence that he used a chemical weapon against the Kurds. So, that question is simply answered.

Did Saddam have a delivery system to get weapons of mass destruction into the United States to attack America with? Well, nineteen hijackers used a method to unleash an incredible amount of damage with not much more than a poor man's "Smart Bomb" with a human guidance system that was never utilized before for their attacks against us.

The nineteen hijackers who conducted the attacks on our country only needed the motivation to be resourceful and follow the basic principles of unconventional warfare to conduct their attack by utilizing their enemy's capability against them. Our enemies were dancing in the street throughout the world, and that attack showed them all the possibilities of what could be. That created more motivation and recruitment for more Jihad warriors. So, we have Saddam on one hand that refused to cooperate with UN sanctions for over ten years and on the other hand he has proven to have WMD with the willingness to use it. Oh, yeah . . . he hates us.

But before America goes to war, our government has to sell it to us. The terrorists that conducted the attacks on 9/11 were Muslim Extremists, and Iraq is not the target of targets for killing Muslim Extremism because Saddam was a secular leader. But Iraq was the easiest strategic sell to the American people so we could get into the region; even though Afghanistan came first, the location of Iraq was more strategic. After all, Saddam did neglect United Nations resolutions for ten years following the Gulf War.

Look at a map of the world and locate the Middle East and you will see that Iraq is centrally located geographically and in the middle of all the areas that promote Muslim Extremist Terrorism focused against America. It was a "no brainer" and that's the end of this chapter.

I wish I knew what else happened in this particular incident, regarding the chemical weapons turn in, because the exploitable non-kinetic opportunities were definitely there and it looks like somebody tried to do a good job.

My PsyOp, My Attitude,

My Behavior

Chapter 10

I'd trained the team on low-light tactics that I learned through training at the SureFire Institute, they could shoot well together on the move, deal with multiple levels of force on force, understand mindset and mental conditioning, and the list goes on. Bill Murphy from Gunsite in Arizona and Firearms Training Associates in California taught me the best of my firearms tactics. He's the best in the business and that's more than a popular opinion, it's a fact. He definitely gets a big piece of credit for the insurance policy that saved my life. Training is a tactical insurance policy. My rule is: pick the right policy for your environment and carry enough ammo to take care of your biggest deductible—keep it simple and get the best instructor.

I study tactics and shooting like some men play golf or watch football; I always have. Whether it's reading Sun Tzu, Clausewitz, or my Ranger handbook, tactics is a language that I understand. The team's tactical skills were far beyond the skills of the rest of the Army and most of the supported units that we were there to help.

Everything I'd learned in the military and years from teaching as a civilian went into their heads. When the owner of a business is willing to pay you for teaching tactics, then I think you've earned the right to truly call yourself a Tactics Instructor, and that's what I actually did with part of my life when I wasn't playing "Armiguy" in Iraq. Getting an instructor certificate from someplace doesn't make anyone a teacher, but it's a good start. I have plenty of "certs" but teaching is a passion. I taught Team Voodoo their tactics and they were beautifully hungry about learning. They were prepared to fight at the drop of a hat and move through events with intention. As far as tactics goes, they and I were squared away. Some things couldn't be taught.

I didn't realize at the time that things I did in my past would come back to haunt me after I got to Iraq and especially after killing a man.

The desire to be on the "right" side of my past turned bad memories into the fire behind an ambition to do good. Throughout my life I always fought something somewhere; as a kid I wanted to be a professional kick boxer. I was the twelve-year-old kid with a double end ball and a heavy bag that had been modified from an old duffel bag that hung in the garage. I had a picture frame with hospital wristbands sandwiched against the glass to keep track of broken body parts. I never thought of myself as a tough guy but I wanted to be and that started when I was young, real young.

In the second grade, I stabbed a kid in the leg with a box cutter on a schoolyard playground. Before that I fought him and beat him up for what seemed to be a week straight. I didn't really want to but I was getting picked on and for some reason this kid deflected attention from me. He begged me not to hit him but then I'd bust his nose or lip. He would cry and I would feel bad inside. After he was taken away in the ambulance I got called to the principal's office and the principal tried to get in touch with my parents. He called my home but nobody was there so he sent a note home with me that I had to return.

I figured that it would be an ass whooping of biblical proportion so instead of giving it to my parents I forged the note with my mom's name and returned it the next day. Can you imagine a second grader forging a note? I might as well have done it in crayon because of course I got caught.

After cutting that kid I didn't have any trouble from kids at school and that created a conditioned response that I could have done without. I learned violence is power; it took a long time to figure out when and how to apply it. My dad applied some power when he eventually found out about the whole thing and I got the belt. I remember him telling me, "Drop your drawers, grab your ankles, and don't you cry"; then I got hit. It was humiliating. I more than deserved to be disciplined for what I did but it didn't hurt that bad and I was used to the belt.

The cops came to the apartment complex where we lived and talked to my mom but I didn't have to go to Juvenile Hall for a crime or anything. I was a kid and it was 1977, so what were they going to do? In a way, I remember thinking, "Big deal, I got the belt; I always got the belt." The important thing was that I didn't get any more shit at school. I was a seven-year-old white kid that was a minority in the neighborhood. I went from getting picked on to practically being a celebrity after the whole incident. That was my first run-in with the law.

Home was never easy for me, it just wasn't. It wasn't horrible; maybe it was just normal and I was the fucked-up one. For me I always wanted to be to "out," growing up. I can't ever remember dealing with rules very well either, not that I was a rebel looking for a cause or way to challenge the established rules. It was the concept of parameters coming from an unworthy source that I had an issue with and I felt like I outgrew everything when I was very young.

I was always the new kid in the class because I went to a lot of schools; either we would move, my mom didn't like the school, or school counselors felt another school in the District was more suitable for me because I was caught with explosives. True story, they weren't really "explosives": They were finger snaps that popped on impact when they were thrown. But in fairness, I shouldn't have been throwing them at the school busses as they drove by. It was always something with school.

I was a special education student and I hated it. I didn't have educational issues either; I was there for behavior modification. I just got bored easy. Today they might call it Attention Deficit Disorder. It doesn't really fit because I typically learned fast and didn't have trouble with concentration. Honestly, I was just bored.

Several grades stayed with the same teacher in a combined classroom. Special education kids were considered the outsider kids that were in "that" classroom that had to visit the regular classes. I sat in the corner because I didn't have my own assigned desk like the other kids and it sucked. It sounds so damn petty now but I look back at that time and describe myself as a young, breathing inconvenience.

Everything changed after the fourth grade. From fourth grade to sixth grade, I had Mrs. Coleman. I loved her. She was so tough on me but I cry when I think of her because she really acted like she believed in me, and I wanted to do anything to please her. It took a lot of time but she was the one that set things straight and stable in my mind about doing good in school. Things smoothed out over the early years. High school was cool and I didn't have trouble there, no more special ed classes and finally there weren't so many rules.

I graduated high school in 1989, turned eighteen soon after, and ended up in an alcohol treatment facility. Now, I think it was just a bad hangover that got out of control. I didn't go home from the rehab, I moved out of my parents' house immediately and in December that year the United States invaded Panama. When I heard that the 82nd Airborne Division had jumped into Panama, I joined the Army the next day.

While I waited to go to basic training I got in trouble for a drunken brawl and then like an idiot I fought the police. I was handcuffed on the floor of a buddy's house and kicked a cop in the balls. That didn't go over well at all. Because of the fight and my drunkenness I had to go to the emergency room on the way to the police station. My dad told the cops that I was leaving for the Army soon and he would make sure I stayed out of trouble until I was gone. No charges were filed but I had to go home with my parents after I sobered up. Going "back home" always sucks when you fuck up. I liked it better than being booked into jail but it was a definite "eat shit" situation.

I waited a month or so and left for Fort Benning. I excelled at the Army stuff. I loved it. I got so much attention and respect in that male high-testosterone environment that I felt like I found a home (how cliché, but it's true). I was an honor graduate in basic training and my dad came out to Benning and pinned my wings on me at my Airborne graduation. That is one of the greatest memories that I have. My parents were happy that I was in the Army, war or no war. Panama was over by the time I got done with Airborne School.

I won't bore you with all the details but after that when I had time off, there were several alcohol-related incidents and fights that landed me in trouble. I even got arrested and charged for punching a first sergeant while I was stationed in Germany, and at Fort Bragg during a 4ᵗʰ of July weekend I got arrested for fighting with the police again. That time I did end up in jail down in Myrtle Beach, South Carolina, for the night; it wasn't so bad. I purposely took a blanket from a guy right in front of everyone and had no problems.

I still excelled at my job in the Army and was promoted ahead of my peers. I was taken care of. The 82ⁿᵈ even expected guys to blow off steam and mix it up on occasion. This was also not a good thing for me, I was still learning that violence is power and safe. I'd matured from that second-grade playground and had learned a little discretion.

During a visit to N.C. State University my buddies and I from Fort Bragg were hanging out looking for college chicks at the local bars. College guys hated that. So there were fights. One night I broke up a couple fights just by reasoning with a few guys. Truth be told, I just didn't want to have to back up my buddy in some silly fight and then not hook up with some girl I met earlier, but I guess it looked like something else. I guess it must've accidentally looked like some cool "Roadhouse" shit.

The club owner or manager saw me and invited me to a back office for a drink. He allowed me to come into his bar whenever I wanted and drink for free as long as I could keep G.I.s from fighting with college students. What a bargain, the trick was I actually had to do what it looked like I did before! So, I came back on the weekends and did it a few times. I liked the protector feeling, it wasn't a new feeling but this was just the first time I'd had it rewarded by another person. It was a pretty easy job because the G.I.s that were causing the trouble were usually my knucklehead friends.

I got out of the Army. I moved home. And soon enough, I was right back where I was just a few months before I left: drunk and handcuffed in front of the cops. It appeared that I couldn't drink tequila without carrying money for bail at the same time. I was in another damn fight.

I scared a liquor store clerk by yelling at him because he couldn't tell me where the fucking Copenhagen tobacco was. He freaked and pointed a gun at me, that was bad, and the fight was on. I almost got myself shot in the process and my buddy shot just for being there. This time I didn't get a free pass. I was nobody special to the cops and I didn't have an Army chain of command willing to stick their neck out for me. I had to go to court. I thought, "Oh shit, now I've got to go to real jail—for a while". It was kind of like my dad telling me way back when to drop my drawers, grab my ankles, and don't cry. This time I was sure that this was going to hurt.

I was nervous in court. Waiting for the judge felt like I was getting a public proctology exam. Sitting in court at my pretrial hearing scared the shit out of me; I was guilty and I knew it. Fortunately, I got an attorney who pled me out to a lesser charge and the judge let me off with a fine. For some reason, I couldn't figure out why this kind of stuff kept happening. I knew that alcohol probably had something to do with it and at that time I was still heartbroken over an old girlfriend from when I was stationed in Germany but I couldn't figure out more than that. I was lost and pushed it all out of my head.

I wandered pretty aimlessly for about three years and worked wherever I could until I did okay financially but I didn't really fit anyplace. I had what I wanted, did what I wanted; I just wanted, I wanted more. Some guys that I knew understood that I was working as a private investigator under somebody else's license and were mistaken about what the actual job meant. Nonetheless, they wanted to pay me to work for them and that sounded like a good idea.

Poor white trash like me at the time didn't mind getting paid, license or no license, for any kind of work. Half the time when I wasn't logging P.I. hours, I was also working as a janitor, window cleaner, bouncer, and anything else that paid money for something I knew how to do.

I wasn't willing to kill anyone and they never asked me to but busting out some windows in a car at a parking lot or tossing a guy through a bread rack at a grocery store didn't seem that bad, they probably deserved it . . . what the fuck did I care anyway? It was money for me and other than a few feelings nothing got hurt.

When I turned twenty-five, I thought to myself that I was going to be forty overnight with nothing to show for it if I didn't do something with my life. Out of the blue I heard about a police academy at the local junior college. I tried to get hired as a police officer when I left Bragg originally but all the local agencies wanted me to put myself through an academy. It wasn't an option then but now it could be.

I set out to get myself into the academy. As for my police record, fortunately for me only one thing after all those years actually ended up on my record. Unfortunately, it just happened to be the most recent event but I was sure that I could explain that away. It turned out that I couldn't but I didn't know it at the time.

I stopped doing the negative things that I was doing, used my G.I. Bill, and enrolled into the academy. I loved it. I learned a lot and what changed me was learning about how there was always a victim for a crime and they needed help. I really hated bad guys.

I never had any ill will for the things I had done and it was never about hurting people. I just liked to fight and everybody I fought with wanted to fight, except for one time. Way back in the second grade when I stabbed that kid, I did that to abuse him—to mutilate and humiliate him. Everything started to change for me from that single realization.

I spent the next three years routinely coming back to that issue on the schoolyard playground as a kid and looking at it. Why didn't I care about the police getting involved, why didn't I care about getting hit by my dad, why didn't I care at all? Since the academy, the people that have come into my life are very focused on their own direction and that's when I began to learn about the strength of my own intellect. I wasted a lot of my life but I wasn't in prison and I had options. *Carpé Diem!* It was time to move on and figure it out while moving forward.

After my last child was born, evidently I became a real teddy bear. She softened my heart so much that I don't have the words to describe it. Around the same time I had a routine doctor's appointment and my doctor asked if something was bothering me. This was a pivotal moment in my life and I don't know how everything happened at once; that happened to be on the day of my appointment for pink eye. If I had been a computer, my hard drive had been broke and had been replaced, files had been transferred but the old software couldn't handle everything so I needed to update and open the old files with new programs.

My doctor had treated me and my family for years and I didn't mind talking to him. He listened and I talked a lot. This was more than just me "growing up," I realized that I had issues (yeah, no shit) and he invited me to join a group involved with self-actualization. I told him that I wasn't into any of that hippie shit and being that he was a former Marine, he understood my sentiment. He explained that is was training and not therapy. Training I could do!

So for roughly the next three years I learned the process and challenged myself to change. I started teaching others how to protect themselves and I was good at it. Before I knew it was 2004 and I had been in this process of this learning for six years with no run-ins with the law or fights. Finally, I got it somewhere. Thank God I did.

I stabbed that kid way back when because I was scared of other kids on that playground. I set out to hurt that kid because he was big but he was weak. He begged me not to hurt him and I did it anyway. After that, it was a conditioned response that continued to revolve in and out of my life.

As much as I had been out of touch, now I was in touch. I had to make it right so I raised my kids strong but with compassion. In Iraq, I can see the fear in people. Just like I felt it in myself and just like I had inflicted it in that kid on the playground. Since I see it in me, I can see it in them and that gives me that ability to communicate it to others, and I know that I can help. It's the right thing to do and must be done. The hardest part is keeping myself in check because getting ahold of Jaysh al Mehdi ignites a visceral reaction to hurt them for what they do.

I have been training my whole life, as long as I can remember I've prepared for fighting. Protecting others by teaching them to protect themselves has been my labor of love for several years. In Iraq, it is so difficult but I can't let them lose this fight or die without a fight. I just can't do it. The whole thing is difficult for me. The team and I work so hard to provide solutions that keep people safe but sometimes it doesn't happen. It really hurts and it especially hurts when we work to point out how people can be helped and they go unnoticed. It's not right. I hate it. I am not a pacifist in any measure. But it doesn't make it easy for me because I came here in hopes of helping with the ability to kill if needed.

In thought and reality, I find it relatively easy to point a weapon at another human being and, when necessary, pull the trigger. I've had to do it and I can do it well. To survive I have to believe I can do it well again and again. I didn't mind killing another human being to complete my mission and I'm not bothered by it but there's a paradox. Killing is not so hard but sharing the death is not so easy. Hearing him pray to live, watching him bleed, trying to ignore his bloody cough, and then realizing he accepted his fate as he faded through to death was odd. I stayed with him until he died.

He and I were so close together when he actually passed away that I could have prayed with him had I thought of it. For me and in my mind I know there was no doubt that it was his life or several of ours. But for some reason when he died, I didn't see the enemy or hate him—I just saw a man.

The death of war was the part that I didn't know how to train for and I failed to train my team for. I wasn't happy that I had prevented our American deaths or horrified that I had killed a person. It was all just "odd" and the situation was visually gross. There is so much death in war every day, I guess the only way to train for it is to practice immediate acceptance without emotion.

Killing has to be done in war and that's the part we can easily train for. We don't do it because we want to, we do it because we have to. Unfortunately, I know oh too well it's dealing with shit after the fact that we don't train for that creates "unwanted bullshit issues" later. Maybe this chapter can be somebody's training when they read it. It's been training to write it. There are parts of our lives that brought us to Iraq and parts of our Iraq experience that we'll bring home.

If there is one thing that I could choose for people to take away from this chapter, it's not my story. We all have a story and the only thing special about mine is that I can talk about some of my own shit in this chapter without too much shame anymore.

I would like people to know that going to war means Warfighters are taking responsibility for actions that leave potential memories others will never understand and they sometimes cause shameful feelings or confusing behavior that may surface in strange ways or pieces over time. Do not judge them too harshly unless you've crawled a mile on their knees. Understand that you can't understand them and they know that, so simply listen with compassion, talk softy, and don't expect too many miracles right away when we come home.

Have your spouse read this if you think it will help. If there is one way that makes us most different: We might seem emotionally hardwired differently. REMEMEBER WHY: "Immediate acceptance without emotion." That was how we all survived—how do we change something that saved our lives and the lives of our team? We're not broken, just different.

An Inability To
Adjust To The Non-Kinetic Fight

Chapter 11

Question: What is the best thing you have seen the current team do?

"They educated the people on the street and explained to them that they had Rights under a Democracy. This team inspired people to stand up and resist the Jaysh al Mehdi Punishment Committee. The people who were Sadr followers understood about what the Punishment Committee did but they began to speak against Jaysh al Mehdi, and the people that were not Sadr followers changed their minds and rejected the tactics of the Punishment Committee. This was a very good thing, courage."

Some say that the United States is always fighting this year's war with last year's tactics. War changes fast. Last week's war is different from this week's war and tomorrow it will be different again. Being able to remain fluid and void of what to expect from the operational environment in combat makes the difference. In reality we can only expect that it is ever changing; everything else is an unforeseen variable. There are no rules, only principles. Accepting the reality and not forcing our expectations is how our team was successful. The good or the bad doesn't make a difference, only the accuracy of information matters. Only acting on accurate information, void of judgment and expectation, can make a difference.

Our ability to adjust at the basic small unit leadership level takes time, too much time, when the military moves like a huge bureaucratic monster, unlike our enemy. Our enemy makes big decisions at the lowest level to achieve maximum effect while we reserve the authority to make comparable decisions for higher levels. Therefore, we are always slightly behind the power curve in keeping up with emerging enemy tactics and opportunities to exploit their weaknesses. They exploit our lag time.

In the military we have various types of operations with desired effects. The operations that desire a lethal effect are called kinetic; basically it is what you see in "war movies." Even though non-kinetic operations may have lethal indirect consequences they are designed to be nonlethal. Non-kinetic operations for lack of a better definition are designed to encourage people to do shit without us being forced to kill them over it or keep us out of hot water when we fuck up.

American forces own a one-on-one street fight, hands down, and the enemy knows they can't win. They have learned that we can overtly hold ground better than just about anyone. But when it comes to the basics of exploiting non-kinetic situations we take far too long to capitalize on the situation, if ever. So we end up not being perceived as well as we could have been or we don't clean up our mess at all.

Most Special Operations units are trained to adjust rapidly and capitalize on environmental opportunities to prop up groups or the populace so we can leave and go home. Conventional forces seize and hold real estate without the focus of using people or groups. Special Operations units treat situations like a rattlesnake, they hit it and go unless it is time to eat, then they pick their meal and maximize it. Conventional forces are more like elephants, they want to graze with other elephants and hang out for as long as they damn well please and have big appetites all the time.

Conventional military forces (some refer to as "Big Army") are trained differently and lose non-kinetic opportunities repeatedly. Conventional military is very focused on order and who has authorization for each specific situation and it should be. However, are they the right tool for this job? Because by the time we get around to sifting through the micromanagement, non-kinetic situational opportunities that require creativity are long gone. Is using Big Army technique the correct method for fighting this war? I don't think so, at least not unless we evolve and mature as a military very rapidly.

In my sometimes-unpopular opinion, we have fought two wars in Iraq. The first portion of the war was to oust Saddam; conventional forces kicked ass and conducted a very kinetic joint operation with Special Operations forces. However, once the invasion was over the environment turned to the low-intensity conflict or insurgent war where Stability and Support Operations (SASO) are most effective. We didn't adjust the mindset of the majority of our conventional forces to look for non-kinetic opportunities. It's not their fault because they weren't trained to adjust. Not adjusting with a more evolved military left us with a limited boots-on-the-ground capability. It underemployed the tactics for the environment.

After the fall of Saddam, Iraq became an environment mostly suited for either better-trained small unit leaders or Special

Operations. Most of the Special Forces were tasked out for high profile kinetic missions that took more skill than the basic Warfighter was capable of. PsyOp teams were tasked out and running very thin, we had 2.5 million people in Sadr City. So, the largest majority of our military strength in Iraq were conventional forces and they hadn't been trained for non-kinetic missions. Most commanders understood the concepts but they were not on the ground beating the concrete every day, and we needed more coverage that could have been conducted by all ground troops. We wasted our troop strength because of a lack of understanding. Rarely would they have had to do anything but be trained enough to recognize opportunities and given the authority to act independently. Collectively it would have put a different face on this war. If we made an error, fine; let's accept it, adjust, and correct it.

The ability to seize the much-needed opportunities by the leaders on the ground became slow and cumbersome. Since they were improperly trained many unit commanders compensated through micromanagement. When I refer to leaders on the ground or small unit leaders, I am referring to the squad leader to platoon leader level tactics, not battalion level. In Sadr City, we had a battalion that was micromanaged by a brigade, and I can say that because I was there and I saw it. How the fuck is a brigade going to be helpful at all in these situations? It appeared that they decided to step on the balls of the small unit leader's authority and creativity rather than get better training or trust the training we gave. Most platoon leaders and platoon sergeants liked having us around on a patrol because for some reason they felt free to make a creative decision—or at least knew they could blame us if something went wrong. I had my "Voodoo balls" in a vise already so I didn't care, much.

Our team trained small unit leaders on how to conduct non-kinetic operations and look for opportunities to influence. There were non-kinetic opportunities but by the time the "think tank" at brigade made a decision and passed down the word to the battalion, who then passed it on again, the opportunity was distant memory. We just can't run this war from the top down.

The mindset was to apply rigid oversight consistent with Big Army mentality. The military has a term called "TTPs," which stands for "Tactics, Techniques, and Procedures." The very concept of needing to rigidly follow a TTP while fighting an insurgency is flawed and plays to the lowest common denominator. I doubt TTPs were designed to remove free thought and limit opportunities. The intent is to standardize actions and methods during certain situations, not all situations. It appeared that since there were no TTP for non-kinetic opportunities then there would not be action taken without some sort of authorization. How can anyone come up with a TTP for every action or reaction?

The mentality creates the lag time that I spoke of earlier. The extreme hesitation gives our enemy an advantage. For example, when Muqtada wants to collect on a bounty offered by Iran to kill Americans with roadside bombs he tells Abu Derra. Then Abu Derra passes out an IED and tells three guys to make it happen and bring back a videotape confirmation so the Militia's PsyOp program can be furthered.

Their mission is well rounded because they nearly always combine their (lethal) kinetic and the (nonlethal) non-kinetic together without all the bullshit. Their kinetic operations are simple, within an open framework and always support a non-kinetic PsyOp program. They maximize their meal when it is time to eat and nothing is wasted. You see that one act will be over in an instant, but they will continually support a campaign around it to affect countless people. I hate to use them as an example but that is a great example of a small unit leader maximizing one opportunity for the non-kinetic fight. While we are employing the latest TTP or trying to figure out what to do if there is not a designed TTP or calling higher for guidance, the enemy had adjusted and moved on. They work within an open framework just like Special Operations are designed to.

All good leaders, conventional forces or otherwise, on the ground applied "principles" not TTPs to create and seize non-kinetic opportunities. However, because of micromanagement, they have little more than a missed opportunity to bitch about when all is said and done.

When a boxer is in the ring and wants to be a successful fighter he can't take his eyes off of his opponent or stop punching in order to turn to his management (who isn't even in the ring). He can't risk getting hit just to ask an opinion about an opportunity. Warfighters who read this will share my frustration regardless of the war they fought. That tells volumes; why have we not changed? Others will say that I didn't understand the "Big Picture" or say that change takes time. Well, they can all have their opinions, and I look forward to reading their book. We have the best military in the world, and it's not because of our technology, as the ignorant say. We are the best because the American spirit drives good people to do their best. I'm doing my best by trying to promote change without being negative and encouraging others. It's just time to evolve and stop confusing strong discipline for stubborn ignorance.

We create, develop, or buy the technology to save the lives of our people on the ground. In return, the hands and motivation of the individual Warfighters do the rest. There is no Yin without Yang. If we train differently we will be different. If we train for the non-kinetic fight, we will conduct the non-kinetic fight and build the populace to choke these bastards out. All Special Operations forces need to get over themselves because they aren't carrying any damn Samurai secrets … share a little more and Big Army will step up and learn more. We all need to collaborate better and drop the egos at the door.

I speak of the men on my team and the men I served with on the ground as if they were my brothers. We have shared the same frustration because we were all forced to take half steps when we should have been at a route step to make good things happen and win the war. Unanimously, the men who fought at a particular place and time during our history say the same thing: "Unless you were there, you can't understand." Well, I know where I was and with whom I served. I take the liberty to speak by saying that we missed opportunities that made a difference and those missed opportunities aided the enemy.

I will say that on a positive side there are many principles that can be derived from the TTPs and we used those principles to be successful. Anyone we served with on the ground can attest to our accomplishments. It would have been counterproductive to follow the step-by-step TTPs, so we adjusted to the environment and applied principles that worked. Our reward was unsubstantiated, constant second-guessing for seizing opportunities that were "off book."

I don't blame those who were doing the second-guessing nor do I hold much animosity towards them because they were trying to be good soldiers, and they did as they were trained. I don't believe this is a problem only with the command I served or my supported unit's higher command; it is a setback with the way segments of the military train and identify success. This is again playing to the lowest common denominator by attempting to run the operations from the top rather than establishing goals, and allowing the small unit leader to accomplish them as they see fit by adjusting to the environment and exploiting all opportunities as they become available in real time.

Big Army uses a flow-chart approach to deal with most things, and that works as long as you have time to continually refer to the chart and the enemy uses the same factors of our flow chart the way we want them to. Small unit leaders need to have the authority to adjust quickly and make decisions to control and manage the space that they own. Kinetic operations are handled well at the lowest level, but the same attention applied to kinetic operations needs to be applied to non-kinetic missions for us to be successful. As much as I hate to say it, the military needs to operate with the same mentality of the lone beat cop back home when it is appropriate. The small unit leadership needs to own their area.

The lone beat cop back home rarely asks permission to make an arrest. Their training and vested authority are all they need, and it is effective. When it comes to non-kinetic operations, remember Boone's simple definition: "Encourage people to do shit without us being forced to kill them over it or keep us out of hot water when we fuck up"; a police officer with six months on the job has more authority to make decisions in America than a patrol leader has in Iraq.

The Civil War 18DEC05

Chapter 12

Question: How do you feel when you see American soldiers kill Iraqis?

"I feel so bad. I wish that this thing never happened and I imagine myself in their place because I am one of them. It makes it worse when they get killed for stupid reasons that didn't make sense. I have been angry with Americans when they killed Iraqis unless they are killed when they were trying to hurt me and the Americans I am with. I am not mad at Americans for killing Iraqis while trying to protect themselves, but during the uprising in Sadr City, some Iraqis were innocent and in the line of fire so they were killed accidentally. I remember some Iraqi soldiers that were accidentally killed by Americans and it honestly made me mad. It is true that it was an accident but good soldiers should not do such a thing."

December 18, 2005 has no major significance in this chapter other than it is the date I started writing it. Prior to coming to Iraq and while studying the culture I wondered how it would be possible for democracy to take hold in an area that was filled with incredible differences and years of infighting. Most cultures and countries develop a desire for democracy through a civil war. How would Iraq be different? Is it possible?

Generally, an alpha group emerges and seeks a new way of life consistent with their beliefs through some form of takeover or envelopment of the existing regime. However, Iraq has three primary groups that are separate from each other and within those groups there are parties that are yet again different. The three groups are Shia, Sunni, and Kurd; none of which had the prowess or power to replace Saddam Hussein's government.

Saddam was Sunni, so Sunnis lost a lot of power by losing Saddam. The Kurds had already staked out their piece of the pie in the 1990s by separating themselves from the main body of the country and taking a large portion of the north. The Shia and the Kurds were persecuted under Saddam's regime but that didn't seem to unify them because Shia have a very strong religious base, while the Kurds are somewhat secular. Other than sharing the same country and being Arab, they all have very different views.

Their differences don't seem like a great combination of factors to help democracy or any other type of governing system flourish. Iraq is very divided. There was no shining group living in Iraq that was able to defeat Saddam. As much as I would love to believe that freedom is easy to accept, I have seen a different reality in Iraq. It kills my American mind to have to accept that freedom is a learned trait here in the twenty-first century. I don't believe freedom can be given as a gift because it has to be earned. I don't believe any person can understand the value of freedom nor can an entire population be willing to defend something they didn't pay for.

A revolution in Iraq, not unlike America, would have defined a central belief worth fighting for and would have created a unifying cause. Simply by natural selection, the most committed ideology with the most committed followers would prevail. However, Saddam was not defeated by a unified Iraqi cause that was paid for with Iraqi blood. The Coalition of the Willing invaded to remove Saddam's regime and then tried to give away the concept of freedom and democracy to the people for the sake of peace. I am a teacher of democracy and freedom in Iraq and they want it once they understand it, but few understand it. The Coalition Forces are still in Iraq to keep the peace as of December 18, 2005, and probably will be for quite some time, or at least the United States should be.

When I speak to people in Iraq and talk to Shia, Sunni, or Kurd, they agree on one thing all the time: When America leaves, it would be bad, and "war between Sunni, Shia, and Kurds will have many deaths." Our team and other teams try to persuade people and get them to acknowledge that they have choices, and that a unified Iraq is the best way to promote a future of peace for everyone. They respond "Insha Allah," which means "God willing." Again, trying to teach democracy in Iraq is like trying to teach dentistry to a boy raised by wolves. It can be done, but it takes time.

Iraqis agree on having Islam as part of their Constitution. Having no separation of church and state can cause a serious problem between the three groups because whose version of Islam is best for the Constitution? That puts the rights of the individual out the door. Individual rights are not something that Iraqis have had the opportunity to absorb. Civil war seems like something inevitable because according to them, only the physical presence of the Americans is preventing it.

I think there will be a war for independence, which we generally refer to as a coup, but first things first. As of right now, I can substantiate evidence of another kind of war for independence that was not foreseen. Muqtada al Sadr has been willing to align with several other Islamic Fundamentalist groups that have not previously been willing to unite, and I believe this will be the first order of business. President Bush has stated that peace from the Middle East hinges on success in Iraq, and he is right from many different angles.

Muqtada and his convenient allies see the same picture as President Bush except from the other side of the fence. I have seen Muqtada al Sadr align with other Shia parties that have previously been enemies, and even with Sunni groups that were enemies. They have all aligned briefly at times but they are far from unified. They unite to kill Americans. Their goal to defeat America doesn't fall under a single leader, only situations of convenience.

Individually Muqtada has the backing of Iran and can get the support of most of the Muslim Extremists in the region to fight Americans; however, he won't do anything to upset Iran's applecart. He may briefly align with his enemies to fight us so long as it doesn't conflict with his Iranian relationship.

All Muslim Extremists around the world would love to see America fail, but they don't have a true stake in the game yet. Losing democracy in Iraq and allowing it to fall would not only be a defeat to the U.S. objective, but it would be a blueprint for success and motivation for defeating America worldwide. The United States losing by pulling out of Iraq too soon would be the absolute worst possible scenario for freedom in Iraq and our security at home. We cannot give up this ground.

Saddam was a prick; however, he destabilized the possibility of an Islamic Fundamentalist superpower in the region and we must do the same because the future success of democracy in Iraq with Muqtada al Sadr at the helm is chancy at best.

By the spring of 2005, Muqtada had twenty Jaysh al Mehdi brigades operating out of Sadr City. All had been put through a four-month training program by Saddam's Former Regime Elements (FREs) and Hezbollah from Iran. Jaysh al Mehdi are not simply "local yokels" with a bad attitude; they are a real army with tremendous capability and have been fully indoctrinated against Democracy. I've spoken to them face-to-face and can identify them most of the time.

They are full-fledged bad guys who want to destroy America by any means possible and they won't stay here in Iraq. For now their mission is to kill Americans in order to influence a withdrawal of troops by creating a lack of U.S. public support and disrupting American operations by removing support of the Iraqi people for long-term peaceful democratic change. The number of militiamen does not include the men who will also follow and simply carry out Jaysh al Mehdi orders. I don't know how many were added to the ranks up to now.

They can be defeated and they will be but we have to do some dirty work, and the American people have to support it. I have brought up Hezbollah and Iran several times. Some of you may be thinking that Hezbollah is from Lebanon and not Iran. Well, this book is generally about what I see and know from being on the ground in Iraq, of course, with some commentary. If you want a detailed explanation of the Hezbollah/Iran connection, then you should read *Tactics of the Crescent Moon* by John Poole, published by

Posperity Press. Mr. Poole has done a great job of explaining it and he should get the credit without me stealing from his work. I can validate what he wrote in his book by the things I observed in Iraq.

Sadly, most Americans don't recognize things they are seeing at the time because they are so far from the war with limited information. Unfortunately, Mr. Poole's book can't offer us solutions (wouldn't that be great!). Reading parts of his book put a wonderful historical perspective to current affairs going on here right now, and I highly recommend it.

It is not even easy to pick a side for a potential civil war or a revolution in Iraq. The psychological dynamic is very complex. If someone were to tell the American people that they would be forced to fight a war and IF they chose the wrong side to fight for, then they would lose their salvation in Heaven. Do you think more people would choose the secular side or the religious side to fight for? That's a psychological dilemma we try to overcome as PsyOp'ers in Iraq.

Muqtada al Sadr is perceived as the one that holds the salvation keys for success over his followers in Sadr City. With twenty trained Jaysh al Mehdi brigades, plus 45% of Sadr City's 2.5 million under the age of fifteen years old and are being indoctrinated in the schools for Jihad, he has influence over a lot of people, and in five years most of those kids will be of military age. You do the math and cut it any way you want.

However you crunch the numbers, they will equal more than the number of the entire Iraqi Army, because many of the Jaysh al Mehdi will also serve in the Iraqi Army at the same time. They will have to choose a side when it comes time to protect the country during a potential revolution or civil war. That is what is in the heads of these fighters, and Muqtada knows it.

These were basic goals that were vital to our safety as Americans, and they are still vital. I am not an officer or politician. I am a sergeant, and that means that I take orders and issue orders to complete the mission. In the absence of orders, I take charge and issue orders based upon the commander's intent and accomplish the mission. I have two directives at all times, which are the welfare of my troops and the accomplishment of the mission. As a non-commissioned officer, my life revolves around accomplishing the mission, so anything not in that purview is of little concern.

If our mission was to oust Saddam, then we accomplished it. If our mission was to establish a legitimate Democratic government, then we have also accomplished it as of now. However, if democracy was for the purpose of helping to secure America, then our security is still in danger.

The key insurgent players responsible for the violence are Sunnis and Shia. The Sunnis attack Coalitions Forces (most specifically Americans), Iraqi Police, and other members of the Ministry of Interior. They attack the Iraqi Police and Ministry of Interior because they know it is an easy way to identify Shia. The Sunni fighters are a few different groups such as Wahhabis, Ansar al Suna, and Former Regime Elements, just to name a few.

The Shia and Jaysh al Mehdi do not attack the Iraqi Police and the Ministry of Interior because they are the Iraqi Police and Ministry of Interior. They control it from the inside and it has been completely saturated by Muqtada's corruption. They also attack Coalition Forces (most specifically Americans) and Sunnis. Primarily, I have seen them focus on Sunni Wahhabis. The Shia insurgent fighters are comprised of Jaysh al Mehdi. The other formidable Shia militant group is the Badr Corps; they are the military wing of the Supreme Council for Islamic Revolution in Iraq (SCIRI). I personally have not seen Badr Corps attack Coalition Forces. Badr Corps and Jaysh al Mehdi don't typically get along even though they both take orders and money from Iran. However, during the 2005 election, they teamed up for voting power and backed the same ticket.

Generally, the Sunnis primarily use vehicle-borne improvised explosive devices (VBIEDs). These are suicide or homicide bombers. Others wear explosive vests to attack the Shia. The Sunnis (mostly but not always) use crude and simple but effective VBIEDs comprised of various-sized artillery rounds. They are effective against civilian vehicles and buildings. They are not very effective against our light-armored vehicles and haven't been great at doing what they planned against our facilities.

When they attacked the Palestine Hotel in late 2005, a soldier with our supported unit from Barbarian Company 3-15 INF, 3ʳᵈ ID stopped it. Specialist Green hosed the VBIED truck with his M240 machine gun, and SSG Brisley, the sergeant of the guard (SOG) during the attack, told me what had happened. I was on leave when it happened and watched it on CNN. All the guys on watch that day deserve being mentioned for doing a great job.

The attack on the Palestine Hotel was the most extensive VBIED attack for a long time, and the Palestine Hotel is very much in the open to hit. It was an enticing target to them because it appears poorly reinforced, but they still failed. The IEDs that Sunnis use against Americans are also simple and crude artillery rounds that are not extremely effective against killing soldiers in our vehicles 100% of the time. So they use them to kill their other enemy, the Iraqi Police, who are Jaysh al Mehdi and who don't have armor-reinforced vehicles.

The Shia and Jaysh al Mehdi currently use a limited amount of VBIEDs because Muqtada wants people compliant and controlled. Limiting VBIEDs gives him the opportunity to look like a protector against the Sunni tactics of indiscriminate killing. The Shia use hit squads to attack Wahhabis because Jaysh al Mehdi smartly attempts to keep collateral damage and civilian casualties to a minimum. Some creative public relations from the Sadr Bureau along with their coercion tactics help them use the people as camouflage, and they can speak bad about the attacks that Sunnis conduct. It is a good way to take the demented moral high ground; Muqtada al Sadr can proclaim that Jaysh al Mehdi only hurts those who deserve it according to Islam and not innocent people at random.

Jaysh al Mehdi's preferred method of killing Americans is the use of specially designed IEDs called Explosively Formed Penetrators (EFPs). The EFPs penetrate the armor on our Humvees and kill the occupants. Muqtada got these EFPs from Iran and they are very effective. I wouldn't be surprised if the Sunnis get ahold of the EFP technology so they can gang up on us.

Sunni and Shia insurgent groups both attack Americans but they do it differently. I know of times when they acted covertly in concert with each other to kill Americans. The occurrence is rare but I would not be surprised if Sunnis and Shia extremists merge more often to create more American deaths until America leaves.

The biggest factor that would impede that happening on a large scale is Muqtada's influence from Iran. If he overtly aligned with Sunnis, Iran would probably pull their support of him unless they initiated it for him. I think that is the most logical reason it has not happened openly and in large scale as of yet. America is an enemy to both of them, and Arabs tend to stick together against outsiders. Again, this is just another indicator of Iran pulling the strings. The Iranian influence for Muqtada al Sadr has been more than a little, and by proxy, Iran is responsible for the killing of Americans in Iraq.

The armed wing of the Kurds is the Peshmerga. Kurds are busy trying to build their country, and I have not seen them involved in the insurgent activity against Americans. They would rather the rest of the country eat itself while they prosper. By the way, if this all sounds confusing, wait a week and it might change. The parts that you can take away that I consider solid information are the complexity of the environment, how the different groups operate for their own goals that are separate from each other, and the external forces that contribute to the chaos. What I have written about here as to who is doing what and with whom is just a snapshot in time from when I was in Iraq.

S.
W.
E.
T.

Chapter 13

American forces established several public services projects to help improve the living conditions and quality of life for the people of Sadr City. We implemented programs to solve problems with their sewage, water, electricity, and trash disposal (S.W.E.T.). A tremendous amount of energy and resources were dedicated to this effort to make the living conditions in Sadr City more livable, but Jaysh al Mehdi influences every action in Sadr City, even when it comes to the people helping themselves. Jaysh al Mehdi had told the people that if they helped the "occupiers" do anything; they would be seen as traitors of Islam and be hurt or killed.

In the movie *Apocalypse Now*, the lead character, played by Martin Sheen, meets up with Col. Kurtz, played by Marlon Brando, and Brando recites his famous "horror" monologue. In that monologue, he describes how he saw a pile of inoculated arms that were cut off of children because they accepted help from the Americans. The same mentality existed in Sadr City. So, the SWET projects received little or no support from the people. Surviving day-to-day and being free from Jaysh al Mehdi coercion meant that the people were going to have to live in sewage-filled streets, and they piled their trash in the roads instead of participating in the trash collection program.

Americans established programs that simply required basic participation in order for them to work. The system was not much different than apartment living in the United States, Germany, or anyplace else. Central collection points were built where it could be picked up weekly but the people couldn't be seen trying to help themselves. So, trash would get piled six to ten feet high outside of the receptacles approximately fifteen away, where it would have to be picked up with shovels by the trash truck drivers. They would rather leave it for the goats to pick through with no regard for the barefoot kids. Jaysh al Mehdi ensured the projects would fail, and that gave them something else they could publicly blame the Americans for.

Would you put your trash in the dumpster if you thought you might get killed over it or leave it for the goats? Everybody was in on the game and there wasn't much more that we could do.

This man is a guard at a small water distribution center co-located with the schools that provide clean water from a few nozzles for an entire neighborhood. The Engineer Staff Officer of 3/15 INF did a great job with these projects but Jaysh Al Mehdi was hell bent on its failure. The reason we were there that day was to tell the people of the area that the water was clean to drink because Jaysh Al Mehdi tried to claim that we were poisoning the people. Also, to make sure that the guard was passing correct info or we would be back and he could lose his job since this was an Iraqi-sponsored facility. Jaysh Al Mehdi even went so far as to break off the nozzles so that people could not get the water. At other sites Muqtada claimed that he had created these resources and that the ones with his posters on them were safe to drink from.

His guards were taking bribes for the water that was created for the people to have for free, just like corrupted water trucks, unless they paid off the driver . . . there would be no water dropped in the 130 degree heat. As a "holy man," how can Muqtada be involved with such shameful acts and he thinks he's unnoticed. The people there know the truth about him and eventually they trusted us, they told us that one day they could revolt over this issue. I wish that it would happen sooner. I wish our support had not been pulled out from beneath them.

It was more than a little frustrating to see children playing alongside sewage running down the street for absolutely no reason. The trash clogged the drainage systems, and so the area became flooded with sewage. The sewage contaminated the drinking water and people got sick and this was a reoccurring issue—all because of the fucking trash problem that would never be resolved because Jaysh al Mehdi forced people to dump it in the street. It wasn't like people were being beaten to death over the issue. It was nothing overt. It was simply understood and they didn't question it.

When Iraqi contractors were hired to repair and build the sewage system, Jaysh al Mehdi exploited that opportunity and extorted money from the contractors to make sure the work was never completed. I have heard of multimillion-dollar contracts being picked to the bone. Each contractor hired a subcontractor, and Jaysh al Mehdi took a portion of the money from the contractor and each subcontractor, until there was simply not enough money to do the work.

Trash trucks were purchased and set up on routes to pick up the trash from receptacles and designated trash collection points, but when the people were forced to not use the collection points, the receptacles did little good to help solve the problem. They actually piled trash around the receptacles but not in them. I think that it meant that they wanted to use them but couldn't. These people tried to do good.

The people knew and understood the cause of the problem and were willing to help themselves but they were not permitted to assist Americans in any way. The drivers of the trash trucks were also not permitted to do their job.

Clean drinking water in the heat of summer was a problem. One time during a patrol, we went into a sector to investigate a point of origin for a mortar attack against our FOB. What we found were people who had not received water for five days. Five days anywhere is a long time to go without water, but in the heat of the Iraqi summer, where the temperature reaches 130 degrees, it is deadly. I asked the people what happened to the water delivery, and they told me that the delivery drivers would not fill the water tanks unless the drivers were bribed. The water program was provided for free to the people of Sadr City from the government, and there was plenty of water, but the drivers were collecting bribes from the poor people of Sadr City and giving it to the Sadr Bureau.

Everything they needed was given to them, and they either couldn't take advantage of it or they had to pay illegal bribes to receive it. Jaysh al Mehdi was behind the extortion of the contractors, and they even extorted the people for water. Very rarely would people step forward and acknowledge the root of the problem, but on occasion, they did and the problem was always Jaysh al Mehdi.

There were District Advisory Councils set up to represent the people, and on the day we found the people of the sector who had gone without water for five days, we went to the DAC to find out their version of the problem. The DAC representative stated that the driver could not deliver to that sector because it wasn't safe for him to stop. The DAC lied about the situation, and within ten minutes, a DAC representative was on the phone with someone from the water station.

Thirty minutes later, a truck had safely arrived without a problem and delivered the water. We were fighting the effects of Jaysh al Mehdi on all fronts. The people of that sector were sick and their children were even lethargic, but still nothing was done to help them until we came along.

133

When we initially went to the sector and discovered the problem, I asked if anyone had gone to the DAC and told them of the problem. As a TPT, we always tried to educate the people by telling them that they had rights and they had a representative who could help. Repeatedly, the people told us that the DAC only took care of themselves. The truth was more that the DAC was infiltrated and controlled by Jaysh al Mehdi. We told the people to organize themselves, drive to the DAC to complain together, and make their representatives work for them. On that day, we went and did it for them but several citizens also went to the DAC.

When we returned to the sector, we were met by the citizens who did organize like we told them to do. They were still holding their filled-out complaint forms in their hands. When they went to the DAC, they were told to leave at gun point and the DAC refused to hear their complaints. Their concerns went unheard, and if American soldiers had not solved the problem for them, nothing would have gotten accomplished. The DAC is supposed to represent the people but they didn't because they were also too afraid of being killed.

One night on patrol, we stopped because shots were fired as we drove by. The patrol turned around and found that a local DAC member had been kidnapped while driving through the city with his wife and young son. Jaysh al Mehdi abducted the DAC member. His tortured, lifeless body was found the next day. We missed the abduction by no more than three minutes, and it happened just after we drove by. I held that man's son, who was inconsolable, as the DAC member's wife wept hysterically. There was nothing we could do for them. Oddly enough, there were Iraqi Police trucks within view that heard and saw nothing. They didn't even respond to the shots being fired.

We told an Iraqi Police Officer to put out a broadcast of the vehicle descriptions we got from the scene. Later, we went to the Iraqi Police Station and they told us that no broadcast was put out and they didn't even know about the abduction. Jaysh al Mehdi controls the DAC and the IPs in Sadr City. Anyone who steps out of line or opposes them is served the same fate. They can be kidnapped, tortured, or killed whenever the Punishment Committee gets the order from Muqtada, and they do it without consequence.

Going to the DAC on the day of the water shortage was only a Band-aid solution, and it is most likely that we only stopped the problem for a short time. For the long term, we hoped to have affected one person who might be willing to stand up and resist them, maybe a mother who had a sick child because of the induced water shortage, or maybe a child who can see for themselves that Jaysh al Mehdi creates problems, and the Americans were there to help. Maybe a child of a slain DAC member could be the new leader of Iraq and oppose the Punishment Committee.

As a TPT, we do what we can to influence as many people as possible to expose darkness and be willing to set themselves free. On the day we returned to that water-deprived sector, we used our loudspeaker and gave a script to a local elder to read, and from his mouth, the people heard a message. They heard him say that the people were victorious and that they were not willing to pay illegal bribes for a gift that was given to them by their legitimate Iraqi government. The people cheered, and our TPT had used the conditions to empower them. That was a good day for Tactical PsyOp and a great day for the people in one sector of Sadr City

Politics And Commanders
Chapter 14

Question: What do you like most about the Americans that you work with?

"I like the way they work and follow through on what they say they will do. They try very hard to do things the way they should be done. They are very educated and have knowledge about many things. They have taught me many things for me to become better. Working with them is like reading a book."

I hope that this book inspires others who were in Iraq to write books and tell their stories because it is good for others to see what happened, and how it happened. Company commanders, battalion commanders, division commanders, and small unit leaders can shed a lot of light on events, experiences, and lessons learned. I would love to see a book written by a Warfighter with the rank of private first class or lower. We should not allow the news to be the only authors documenting our recent history as Americans.

The news tends to report a macro overview but rarely has access to the micro events that lead to success or failure. Information gets filtered and obscured, with good reason, because no media organization can cover everything. I would like to say that even though I write about topics like "Our Inability to Adjust," and have probably told more about atrocities that appear to have been overlooked concerning Jaysh al Mehdi and Muqtada al Sadr, I place no blame towards my government's strategy and have no regrets for my service. I served in an all-volunteer Army to defend my country and help the people of Iraq. I think that President Bush's administration has done a great job fighting the War on Terror and the war in Iraq.

Politics and peaceful means should always be completely exhausted before we unleash the dogs of war. All life is sacred but there is a time for war, and Iraq was, in every way, a just war. There has been a lot of second-guessing about how our government handled the war, and if there is any second-guessing to be done, it should be for how some commanders conducted their units, which is my point of view. The truth is that there is no 100% solution for success and nothing is perfect. Now that I have identified my position of who I support, I will also belly up to the bar and explain what I do not agree with.

I do not agree with commanders who act like politicians and make decisions to not fight the enemy, and end up limiting Warfighters from a committed fight when we have the means to fight. This does not save lives nor does it bring peace. It gives opportunity for the enemy to achieve their objectives. I put my men in harm's way, and we were forced to allow the enemy to go unpunished for violence or potential violence against American forces and against the Iraqi people, who could not help themselves. There were people who tried to kill my men and had the means to do it. Not punishing them for those actions only condoned their behavior.

We gave Sadr City to the Iraqi Security Forces in December of 2005, and prior to that, we experienced a systematic restriction of operations against the enemy. That systematic restriction culminated with roving patrols only on the perimeter, and we were ordered not to dismount from the Humvees.

On the surface, it appeared that we were restricted so Sadr City would seem peaceful and ready to be turned over. There didn't appear to be any enemy activity but only because we weren't allowed to look for it or deal with it. Sadr City was the command and control area for Jaysh al Mehdi, and we gave it up first. Our FOB was the first FOB east of the Tigris River to relinquish control to Iraqi Security Forces. I will admit that I do not know the good reason for this. However, I do know that the primary objective during tactical operations is to seize control of the command and control areas of the enemy. Why we gave that up, I do not understand.

We were reassigned to a new unit responsible for the area east and southeast of Sadr City. Our new unit was new in country, and Sadr City was their area of interest but it was not their area of operation. The Sadr Bureau called a meeting with the new supported unit commander as a meet and greet.

In the chapter "Tactical PsyOp Today," I discussed some of what took place at that meeting with the new supported unit's command and the Sadr Bureau just prior to the Summara bombing. That meeting took place on February 11, 2006; I was invited only as an observer to that meeting with top Sadr Bureau members in Sadr City. I heard from them what we all suspected.

According to my old buddy Saed Kareem al Bukahti, the previous brigade commander that was responsible for the battalion in Sadr

City was running the war in Sadr City from a cell phone, where he was calling the Sadr Bureau. Then everything made sense about why I got so much grief and that brigade commander "thought" he knew everything. That bitch got played and could have got my men killed because of it! The Sadr Bureau requested that the new unit have the same "deal" as they had with the previous brigade commander.

The Sadr Bureau wanted no operations conducted without their prior knowledge. Additionally, they wanted all Jaysh al Mehdi members released from the unit's detention facility. Of course Saed Kareem did all the talking and told us that the Sadr Bureau was able to contact the previous brigade commander by phone when there was a problem, and he would take care of things in the past. They made threats of walking away and not keeping the peace if they couldn't get the same "deal" now. The new supported unit commander didn't know how to handle them effectively. He was just too "off-theme" so he didn't appear strong and competent like Lieutenant Colonel Luck did.

On the surface, I wouldn't normally believe the allegations about Lieutenant Colonel Luck's old boss, who was our old brigade commander. I don't believe everything I hear from the Sadr Bureau; however, I was in Sadr City during that time and experienced those situations and that made their allegations seem credible. Saed Kareem said things that I remember happening. I remember when we became restricted from arresting Jaysh al Mehdi members. I also remember when we were restricted from conducting nighttime raids, and these were the same requests that Muqtada's representatives wanted from the new supported unit commander. I didn't envy him during the meeting because he was between a rock and a hard place. One of the Sadr Bureau members told us that Americans had "conducted their last attack in Sadr City," and it sounded like a threat to me. They also advised us that they no longer allowed low-flying helicopters. It doesn't take a general to figure out what was behind that request. We had a serious problem because we had already given up the ground in Sadr City, and taking it back again would be a difficult task because Muqtada would be able to promote the appearance of American forces as being "occupiers" and not "liberators."

Saed Kareem al Bukahti and me that day. He and the rest of the Sadr Bureau were very arrogant the day of this meeting. I think they showed up with a loaded deck. I think their only purpose was to "test" the new commander in charge of the area and see what would happen when they pushed him.

If Americans are seen as "occupiers" then retaking Sadr City would cause a bloodbath and would start the whole war over again from the beginning. Muqtada and his Sadr Bureau leaders were adamant about keeping Americans out of the city and they were willing to fight for it. This security concern should have been the job of the Iraqi Security Forces, but the majority of them worked for Muqtada, and if he gave the order to abandon their posts or turn a blind eye to Jaysh al Mehdi operations, they would. I know this because I talked to them on several occasions. They told me that they followed Muqtada above all others, and if he told them to desert their posts, they would. It is the duty of every member of Jaysh al Mehdi to get a legitimate job working for the Ministry of Interior. We were hung out to dry.

Today is February 13, 2006, and I have no idea how this will play out but I can honestly say that Muqtada al Sadr has the most control over the densest insurgent-infested piece of property in the entire country. He has the freedom and safety to operate outside of our purview, and I am sure that he will take it all. The Cav did the fighting in Sadr City during the first uprising and they deserve the credit for doing a fine job. They killed an estimated 1,500 Jaysh al Mehdi before it was over. Saed Kareem was one of the men who helped negotiate the peace in Sadr City. Once the Cav left and 3rd ID took over, Muqtada al Sadr used his energy to take over the government organizations like the Iraqi Police and members of the Ministry of Interior. He was eventually able to run the city with a corrupted mob-like order and balanced his Punishment Committee operations, which went untouched by tainted officials. He was not this entrenched before the uprising and Jaysh al Mehdi fought hard. Now he owns it all. It is the politics of the commander that are making the facts look successful. In actuality, because he held us back the outcome of the enemy's increased combat power has become the true reality.

Bombing Of The Golden Shrine

Chapter 15

This chapter is dedicated to 2ⁿᵈ Platoon (Night Hawks) Charlie Company 2nd Battalion of the 108ᵗʰ Infantry Regiment National Guard, from New York. On Easter Sunday, 2004, they were attached to the 1ˢᵗ Infantry Division and attempted to avoid this same Golden Shrine out of respect for a Shia holiday and were ambushed, resulting in the loss of Private First Class Nate Brown; seven other men of the platoon were wounded.

There was a bombing of a Shia shrine in the city of Samarra, Baghdad, in February of 2006, soon after our meeting with the Sadr Bureau. The shrine was not just a mosque or place of worship for the Shia, but it truly was a shrine where two of the original Imams were buried. This was an ugly defilement of a legitimate holy site, and it sparked tremendous violence throughout the country. The original report stated that Sunnis committed the bombing. Jaysh al Mehdi used the situation to further their hatred towards American forces and issued information to all Shia that Americans committed the crime with the help of the Sunnis. Jaysh al Mehdi claimed that they observed Americans in Humvees go into the shrine just prior to the explosion.

This was another far-fetched lie designed to separate the support of the populace from the only true protectors of the people in Iraq. For several days following the attack on the shrine, Jaysh al Mehdi ignited sectarian violence and attacked, kidnapped, tortured, and killed hundreds of Sunnis in our area of operation. My team was sent back out to Sadr City to help and act as a forward "on call" element to attempt to stem the violence. I contacted some good people that I knew in Sadr City to report on the situation and learned that the situation in Sadr City was worse than any other place in Iraq, and that Jaysh al Mehdi had Sadr City under siege. Our team provided the information we learned to the Tactical Human Intelligence Team, and they submitted an Intelligence Report to the division headquarters as if the source reporting was their source; what a great move because the truth is that they had no sources in Sadr City and our command wasn't interested in ours. So we worked together and within four hours, all of the forces in Baghdad were deployed to stop the violence and the country was under a curfew. It is hard to regret doing something that saved potentially hundreds of lives; some non-kinetic follow-on operation would have made it even better and really seized some great opportunities.

The following is sterilized information that went to our supported unit commander along with our assessment. This information is the same that went to division headquarters with the THT minus the assessment. Here is what the report looked like based upon the information we received from our contacts in Sadr City:

Sir:

I have attached a slide with general information regarding tonight's events. This e-mail is comprised of the specific information from today. At approximately 1500 hrs today, I spoke with a man that lives in Sadr

Boone Cutler

City. He and I have excellent rapport that was established from previous operations while we were operating out of FOB Hope. Our friend reported the following Atmospheric info and Passive Intel:

- **** was in charge of security operations for Shia Imam Shrines. He had deployed with several members of the Jaysh al Mehdi to conduct the security throughout Baghdad.*
- *Muqtada al Sadr is giving Orders through ***. The current Order was for Jaysh al Mehdi to kill Sunni Wahhabis.*
- *Last night, 22FEB06, in Sadr City 22–28 Wahhabis were killed in the streets of Sadr City. Their bodies were left in the streets "like dogs" for the people to see them.*
- *The following morning at 1100 hrs, Jaysh al Mehdi ordered the Iraqi Police to take ambulances around and retrieve all the dead bodies and take them to the ***.*
- *Muqtada al Sadr ordered Jaysh al Mehdi to not shoot at Americans and to "hold their weapons." He told them that if they shot at Americans, it would be harder to get a job as an Iraqi Police Officer or Iraqi Army Soldier because they need a Recommendation Letter from the United Islamic Coalition and Jaysh al Mehdi. Muqtada al Sadr warned that if they shot at Americans in Sadr City that they would not get their Recommendation Letter.*
- *There is a standing Order that was reiterated for Jaysh al Mehdi to not allow each other to be detained by American Forces. It appears that even though Muqtada al Sadr doesn't wish for Jaysh al Mehdi to engage Americans in Sadr City, he does sanction the lethal engagement of Americans to avoid capture.*

- *** lives in Sector *** near the Hospital and does not have license plates on his vehicles.

- Sheikh *** is responsible for all the kidnapping and stealing of cell phones. He lives in Sector ***. Sheikh *** is a high-ranking Jaysh al Mehdi member. Our friend in Sadr City can positively identify the home of Sheik ***.

ASSESSMENT: Since the evening of 22FEB06, it appears that Jaysh al Mehdi is obviously reacting strongly to the explosion that occurred at the Shia Shrine. I believe that Jaysh al Mehdi operations will continue to expand if they are not opposed. The people in Sadr City are reportedly very afraid and attempting to remain neutral and out of the Jaysh al Mehdi's way. Originally, *** had publicized that the Americans were responsible for the damage at the Shrine. According to our friend, most of the people didn't honestly believe it; however, the Jaysh al Mehdi used it as an excuse to conduct and justify operations. The rumor of Americans conducting the attack on the Shrine didn't last through the night. The people do still have faith in us.

At 2140 hrs, I spoke to our friend in Sadr City again and he reported very good information. The most alarming information is that the Order to kill Wahhabis had been expanded to include ALL Sunnis. Here is the information we have so far:

- *** was issuing Orders for Muqtada al Sadr by *** to the local Jaysh al Mehdi commanders in Sadr City.
- All the people are afraid and doing their best to stay indoors. There is still a lot of shooting and killing going on.
- Jaysh al Mehdi member *** is responsible for the security of Sector *** where *** lives and where the Orders from Muqtada al Sadr are coming through.

145

- *** is giving the Orders from his home where he lives in Sector ***, Mahallah number ***, Street number ***, House number ***/***/***.
- The Jaysh al Mehdi member issuing the Orders has a brother that lives with him and his brother drives an olive colored ***.
- ***, the Jaysh al Mehdi member issuing the Orders, rotates his vehicles but has been known to drive a *** and an ***. He does not use a license plate sometimes.
- ***, the Jaysh al Mehdi member issuing the Orders, home is described to be a two-story home with two white doors.
- Our friend can positively identify the home of ***, the Jaysh al Mehdi member issuing the Orders.
- At some time since our last conversation at 1500 hrs, the Order to kill Wahhabis had been changed. Since the Jaysh al Mehdi went unopposed, the Order was given to start killing all Sunnis, not just the Wahhabis. The Order was given to "round up" all the Sunnis.
- The Order was to kidnap Sunnis and take them into Sadr City where they could be executed at soccer fields. Our friend heard from others that this Order was being carried out. He did not know the specific location of which soccer fields were being used.
- These Orders are being given by Muqtada al Sadr.
- At approximately 2130 hrs, Sunnis were killed on the road leading into Sector *** from the town of ***.

ASSESSMENT: I asked our friend to tell me the general atmospheric sentiment of the people in Sadr City. He explained that the people don't have any control. They don't like these killings but they are powerless. The Jaysh al Mehdi is openly carrying weapons and claiming to be protecting them because the Sunnis are bad and trying to destroy the Shia. They don't actually believe it; however, they don't have an opportunity to stand up against them because they will be killed as collaborators if they try. It appears that Jaysh al Mehdi is exploiting the opportunity to kill as many Sunnis as possible until the Jaysh al Mehdi is stopped. The Iraqi Army and the Iraqi Police are working for the Jaysh al Mehdi and they don't appear to have the ability or will to stop Jaysh Al Mehdi operations.

The concern is the kidnapping of Sunnis that live in our Area of Operation. From a PsyOp perspective, if this occurs in mass, it will be hard to overcome, and losing the people's trust could result in increased attacks against Americans with less reporting of these crimes. It will give the Jaysh al Mehdi a stronger hold on the area.

Yesterday, Sistani and Muqtada al Sadr spoke publicly about a time of mourning for the losses and asked the people to stop fighting. However, privately it appears that Muqtada al Sadr has ordered the attacks to continue as well as expanding the target of the attacks. This can be substantiated by the ongoing and increased attacks. I have not seen attacks continue after a time for mourning was declared and I believe that Muqtada al Sadr is exploiting the lack of troops in Sadr City to carry out these attacks.

I asked our friend what he thought we could do to stop the attacks and regain the trust of the people which did not include re-occupying Sadr City. I have to give him credit for his insight during our discussion. If we deploy American Forces to secure the Shia Imam Shrines and show good faith towards the Shia people, we might be able to regain the trust of the people and defuse Muqtada's justification for the killings. Of course, this Course of Action could expose us to attacks but either way we will probably be attacked. From a PsyOp perspective, we have a better chance to keep their trust, demonize Anti-Iraqi Forces, and stop more attacks if

147

we are seen as their "protectors." A strong Information Operation and PsyOp Campaign as protectors of Democracy could put a lid on this if we back it up with protecting the Shrines and take that security out of the hands of the illegal Jaysh al Mehdi.

Sunni Extremists will not allow this to continue and of course we are all concerned with being in the middle of their retaliation. If a Shia and Sunni war starts, we will be in the middle because Shia Jaysh al Mehdi working for the Ministry of Interior and Ministry of Defense will stop going to work and leave the country unprotected while they fight for Muqtada. I think we, as your TPT, can help you avoid this potential outcome.

As always, I am available at your convenience. Have a good day.

Thirty minutes after I sent that e-mail, our team was sent to FOB Hope in Sadr City for the next five days. We couldn't get into the city. At least we were forward of most units and had a chance to make contact. I wasn't willing to take the team in the city because Americans were not going into the city and going with an Iraqi Army escort was advised against by our interpreter. I had to trust him and we knew that the Iraqi Army couldn't operate for shit. Our language barrier between the security element and the Target Audience would create too many unknown factors to deal with, there's a fine line between having sack and being stupid.

We needed to be creative, so for five days we made loudspeaker broadcasts from over the FOB wall and into the city. We asked people to call in so we could talk to them. Then came a quick assessment through some general questions and a tailored message.

Here is a bit about some good PsyOp. If I say to everybody as they call in that Americans are coming to kick ass if Jaysh al Mehdi doesn't stop killing, I need to back it up or everything that comes over the loudspeaker will be seen as crap and a lie. However, if I ask how people are doing and empathize with them, I create rapport, then say that I think the good people should do their best to stay inside if they see Americans coming because these murders are wrong . . . I convey a messages of compassion, sincerity, and strength. And I do it without saying the Americans are coming and lose my credibility. Now, I have their attention and I can cater to the whispered truth over the phone.

The best PsyOp'ers develop three-dimensional messages and not simply statements. We lose too many non-kinetic opportunities that die on the vine. That time back at Sadr City was a defining opportunity for the creative non-kinetic fight and the guys that do it right not only know the job but they know themselves. Here is my "hippie shit" commentary: It comes down to the basics; embrace reality and the facts rather than denying truth, be spontaneous, be interested in solving problems that may include personal problems or emotional conflict with others, and accept yourself and others with a lack of prejudice. I don't buy into all of it, but the basics are pretty dead-on for me. All these things lead to creativity and touching people in a way to influence their attitude is our job. But you can't do it, if you don't have it. The best PsyOp'ers have it.

We also spent time with the Iraqi Army soldiers who wanted to go into Sadr City and stop the violence. During those five days, the killing continued in Sadr City and Jaysh Mehdi had the city completely locked down. But one day, some Iraqi Army soldiers that we spoke to on the front bumper of our guntruck decided to make a difference and shot up some of the Mehdi during a patrol when they tried to push them around. I was so proud. Chesh, Nacho, and Frank all spoke to those guys and they did a great job . . . no, not just great, fucking great!

I estimate, after talking to Iraqi soldiers and interpreters, that more than 500 Sunnis were killed inside Sadr City after being kidnapped. I don't have any Impact Indicators from the calls that we received from our loudspeaker broadcasts, I don't know if we helped. So our TPT can't put a feather in the cap for that one but it was an opportunity that the entire team handled well while under a tremendous amount of pressure. That is enough success for me.

At that time, there were only about twenty American soldiers on the FOB who were dedicated as an FOB Quick Reactionary Force (QRF) and the Military Training Team (MiTT) that were assigned. The few good Iraqi Army soldiers around told us that they were not afraid to fight Jaysh al Mehdi and proved it, but out of the 900-man Battalion, many of them were working and reporting for Jaysh al Mehdi. More than one Iraqi soldier told us that he was afraid to act or say anything against Jaysh al Mehdi because Jaysh al Mehdi had the power to order Iraqi Army officers to turn over their soldiers to Jaysh al Mehdi to be killed. Jaysh al Mehdi was running the entire city and nobody formidable opposed them. Hopefully, we helped a little.

The War Back Home

Chapter 16

The war seen back home is a touchy subject because the bulk of what America knows is what the news reports. When I first saw this mural painted on the streets in Sadr City that we were protecting, I wanted to hate all Iraqis and just go home. We liberated "them" from Saddam and this is their sentiment. We saw many murals like this and many times done with an American flag next to an Israeli flag. I was angry but I was also ignorant. I had a lot to learn about "learned helplessness" and the Hezbollah influence being pushed through Jaysh al Mehdi onto the Iraqi people. I hope this book helps wipe away some ignorance others may have. I don't mean "ignorance" as a derogatory term; the truth is that our information at home is very limited, not by design, but because of difficulty. Our team had been on operations and at the exact place when things happen and when we saw the news reports on the event, they were way out in left field. Of course, not all the time but it happened more than not, and they were not even tracking on Sadr City. Even the so-called military experts whom I have always felt were so rightfully respected were incorrect. The truth is that unless you were there, you are doing little more than guessing.

During my tour in Iraq, the sentiment in America over our involvement in the war changed, and we felt it in Iraq. The Bush administration was under heavy fire to rejustify the war, and the people wanted answers. When I left for Iraq, most everyone didn't like the fact that we had to be at war. There were some hawks amongst us, very few doves, and for the most part, it was accepted as a necessary evil. The Democratic Party failed to make unjustified war messages stick to the ribs of most Americans during the Kerry vs. Bush for President Campaign, and President Bush won. But in late 2005, they were spinning their wheels again. Democrat and presidential alumni Bill Clinton even came out and made his Monday-morning-quarterback speech about how the Bush administration handled the war irresponsibly.

Most people criticize what they don't understand, and when I went on leave in October of 2005, I spoke to a lot of people. I hadn't planned on it, and I would have rather been left alone. I was on leave, and the last thing I wanted to talk about while on leave from a war — was war. However, I heard a perspective that was way off-base and even my good friends seemed doubtful. This was a war that I was fighting and I actually knew about the good things happening. I was there and heard the people of Iraq express appreciation, and many yearned for freedom.

Our team had helped capture insurgents, and they were on the run. I read the Intelligence summaries every day. I had been on several raids and cordon and searches in Sadr City and other places in Baghdad, so I knew the fruit of our labor was filled with goodness. I had survived an ambush and seen a lot of innocent people killed at the hands of the enemy. Americans were killing and disrupting enemy activity every day. It could have been better but we weren't sucking either. Good Americans were being wounded and killed, and innocent Iraqis were being killed, but we were helping them. It was tough but we were winning by every measurement I could see.

Courtesy Of: I.P. Gonzales

Our team captured this man for allegedly being a weapons trafficker in Sadr City for Jaysh al Mehdi. Nobody in America heard about the event. The rules say that I can't show his face and techically I should say 'allegedly'; I agree with it, even though I would like to expose him more. That is the difference between them and us: We care about individual rights.

These captures happened often and were done at the risk of many lives. But still our country was losing support in us. It hurt us bad. We were doing a good job. This man was a dangerous insurgent; however, since his name was not Zarquawi, it just didn't matter. He has arms, they are just comfortably zip-tied behind his back.

Vietnam was Vietnam and America left Saigon in 1975, but I was hearing people refer to Vietnam's situation when talking about Iraq. However, they are very different. Perception is reality, and America's perception, plain and simple, was being shaped by the news reports that they heard and saw. When I spoke of the war and said what was going on, nearly everyone told me that if they had heard what I said, that their opinion would be different, and I needed to tell others what I told them. That is the reason I decided to write this book and try to do what they asked.

I don't claim to be a terrorism expert or an investigative reporter. I am only a simple man with eyes that see, and this book is about what I see and know from serving in Iraq during the war. The positive and the areas that need improvement are here for the world to judge. I don't think that the Democrats control of all the media, and neither do the Republicans, but if either party talks about something new, it will make the news.

The story of Americans becoming victorious seemed to not make the news because that information was no longer new or interesting. The Democratic Party needed to set an agenda for the next election so they started using the old Vietnam story lines, and that was newsworthy. I am not saying that the Republicans would not pull the same tricks if the tables were turned, but I will say that I doubt the discussion would have ever even existed because I don't think there would have been a commitment to fight the enemy if a Democrat would have been in office during 9/11.

Airing opinions about controversial subjects makes the news for the same reason I flip from the History Channel to watch "The Jerry Springer Show" late at night. I love the History Channel and I have been known to watch it for three hours at a time, every night for weeks on end. But sometimes I want to see two groups of opinionated people argue about who is more stupider'er, even if they are ridiculous. When Beavis slaps Butthead, I find it funny, and the same goes for watching politics at times.

When I was home on leave, the things I heard on the television and radio were negative statistics about the war. I asked the other guys who had already been home on leave if they experienced the same, and they did. I suspect it was a common sentiment among Warfighters coming home, and it's heartbreaking. Again, perception is reality, and all I heard was statistics, not stories. I knew the stories, so my perceptions were different. The reality is that statistics can prove anything you choose, and people love to throw numbers around to prove their point. So, the Democrats are using the Vietnam story line, and the media was providing statistics to show the parallels because it was simply news that got people to tune in.

There are a lot of fifty-/sixty-something-year-old people who watch the news and vote, who remember the Vietnam era clearly, and are afraid of that scenario repeating. That was a great play by the Democratic Party, and it was nothing more than a political tactic to achieve a goal, but it had a secondary negative effect on us in Iraq.

I am doing my best not to show the colors of my political affiliation but I am also not shy of saying what I observed in Iraq that was consistent or not consistent with what I heard on the news. One day, I was eating in our wonderful Chow Hall (I say that with complete sincerity because we had a wonderful Chow Hall on our FOB in Sadr City, and it doesn't surprise me that the KBR employee was a former Division trooper), when I saw an episode of "The O'Reilly Factor" on television. Mr. O'Reilly was having little more than a spat with former talk-show host Phil Donohue.

Mr. Donohue was promoting a peace march in Washington, D.C., as he slammed the Bush administration by using the old Vietnam story line, and Mr. O'Reilly argued his point. Mr. O'Reilly was on track with the things I saw in Iraq; hands down, that is simply the truth. I don't usually watch "The O'Reilly Factor," and that was the only episode I had ever seen from beginning to end. Therefore, I don't know all his views, but on this day, he was sharing the sentiment that I felt, and I would like to thank him for that one day.

My team and I felt a significant slowdown during this time when the American people were demanding a rejustification for the war, and we stopped hunting the bad guys. Actually, I felt more like we were being hunted. For a time, we took the pressure off and our enemy put their best foot forward. During the movie *Blackhawk Down*, the character General Garrison makes a statement about "losing the initiative" when he realizes his men were overwhelmed because they were reacting to the situation rather than controlling it. That's what was happening to us, and we could see it for ourselves everywhere.

We had the enemy on the run and then we just downshifted and they took us on the inside lane. I don't have 500 pages of data to show these facts and that is my disclaimer, but I do know that the American people on my block were getting freaked out by the body count being reported. We had gone from 1,900 dead Warfighters to 2,000 and then 2,100 very fast, and that information without the stories behind it was damaging to operations being conducted in Iraq. There's a lot of information behind those numbers that was not told. We were paying the price for success and doing a good job. America was getting the statistics but not the stories.

The loss of life fucking sucks. Every American who died in Iraq had a family somewhere back home. There was someone who loved them, and they will feel an unyielding emptiness because of that loss forever. No holiday will ever be the same and no family event will be complete. Their home will be forever changed and their photos will be cherished in a way like never before. Nothing will ever be the same for those families. However, this is war; it's not called "dating." It is because of home and family that we serve, and we do so knowing that we risk being killed. There is not one American Warfighter who died in Iraq and did so for nothing. I despise every word written or spoken that insinuates such a vile misrepresentation of the real facts.

The Jaysh al Mehdi operates in Iraq, but it cannot operate inside America the same coercive way because our people know what freedom is, so we are not susceptible to their tactics. But they and the rest of the terrorists around the world can and will affect America from the outside if the Warfighters are held back. Americans have a right to free speech and rightfully we should. It is part of our wonderfully designed Constitution. Any American can write a book and sell it. We have cable television, satellite television, and the Internet. You name it and it can be broadcast every way possible.

The right to freedom of speech and having a free press is essential for the success of freedom. As an American paratrooper, I will even defend your right to burn the American flag. However, I might choose to kick your ass if you try it in front of me, but I'll defend your right to do it. We are a beautiful nation, and if you don't believe it, just talk to a veteran or immigrant who has seen a war-torn country that was ravaged by a dictator.

Those who died in Iraq are all heroes, and I don't care if they died in the heat of battle, were blown up by an IED, or choked in the Chow Hall. The bottom line is that they were in Iraq, not at home, and those American Warfighters were in Iraq carrying a weapon on foreign soil to protect our home. If they were serving, they died doing a hero's duty and deserve every honor that can be bestowed upon them. "Support the troops" has become a buzz term for this war but expressing support for the troops but not the mission, in my view, is a cop-out. The vast majority of us who served in Iraq support the mission wholeheartedly, and who knows better than the Warfighter on the ground?

Supporting the mission is the only way to support the troops. Otherwise the operational downshift in the tempo that occurred will occur again, and we lose more troops in the long run when America doesn't support the mission because it motivates the enemy.

The Psychological Effect Of Resolve
Chapter 17

President Bush spoke a lot about "resolve" in the early days after 9/11, and he did for good reason. In America, we typically think of time in terms of weekly, monthly, semiannually, or annually. It seems the longest we have to wait for anything is a four-year presidential term of office. We, myself included, have a different concept of time than our enemy, and in 2005, America started expressing that it was time for war to end.

Our enemy capitalizes on our perception of time. Ho Chi Minh did it and he set the stage of learning for this enemy. That is one parallel I don't mind drawing to Vietnam, but it is also the one factor that we control at home and not on the battlefield. America focuses on achieving a tactical victory in the most humane way possible, or else we scorn our leadership with pointed fingers.

Our enemies around the world focus on a long-term strategic victory over time, and humanity or guilt is not a factor. America has not lost a single tactical battle in Iraq or Afghanistan, but strategically, as long as we choose to consider a tactical victory as a supplement for defeating the enemy, we will set ourselves up for failure. Our enemy has time on their side, and they have schools to propagate hatred for the American culture generation upon generation, and time is not a factor. They can wait and take a bite at a time. Over time, they will defeat us if they continue to unify while we divide ourselves and lose our resolve. And that is a Boone Cutler guarantee. The world is full of countries with overt or covert Islamic armies that are poised to do whatever it takes to hurt America, and their clock turns a lot slower than ours.

They have been at war with us for almost two decades, and maybe longer, and we simply haven't accepted it. Even now, we would like to believe it is something other than what it is; we call it a war over ideology but for them, clearly, this is a Holy War. Releasing our "can't we just get along" fantasy and acknowledging that we are in an ugly battle for our existence is unbelievable for most but it is reality.

Muqtada al Sadr is building powerful allies to establish and facilitate the first Islamic superpower from all over the smaller Islamic countries around the world, who can be played as pawns on a chessboard. His intention is to facilitate the Day of Judgment because he believes the Imam Mehdi will return and create a one-world universal Islamic government.

In WWII, we defeated Nazi Germany and the rest of our enemies. Japan laid down their arms when the Emperor unconditionally surrendered but they both played by the rules of conventional warfare; still we had to get real dirty to finish it. We weren't alone; America didn't win WWII by ourselves, and our Allies deserve credit, too. I have never met anyone who feels bad about our victorious outcome. There is nothing wrong with winning, and we win when we are united.

Today's enemy doesn't even exist on a map because Muslim Extremists live within peaceful countries. There is no ground to take, and we are not prepared to kill everything taller than your knee in every Islamic country around the world, and nor should we. Even if we did occupy every Islamic country, they would nibble at our toes until our legs were gone. It is necessary to accept this war for what it is and not deny the existence of a Muslim Extremist Holy War with America. The vast majority of Arabs and Iraqis are peaceful; this is no different than every German was not a Nazi. An Islamic Fundamentalist may only wish to control their region but Muslim Extremists like Muqtada al Sadr and his allies want to rid the world of everything non-Muslim.

This is a long-term, very dirty war with no borders, and when we simply choose to abandon all the self-imposed guilt that keeps us from fully committing to do what must be done, only then can we put the specialized Warfighters where they need to be and allow them to be absolutely successful. Sadr City had one Tactical Psychological Operations team dedicated to its 2.5 million-person population. My team was made up of three to four men, who worked in the heart of Jaysh al Mehdi. We needed more time before we got pulled out.

America has, if need be, the ability to create the military units and government agencies that will defeat Muslim Extremists and terrorists like Muqtada from the inside. I have seen the susceptibility of his followers, and he is not without an Achilles' heel. Removing his support of the populace is the key and it can be done. I doubt that any of his counterparts are much stronger than he, but the longer we wait, the harder it will be. Day by day, more become indoctrinated and coerced beyond the point of return.

Truth is on our side, and human nature could defeat him if we allocate our commitment. The time to accomplish this mission against the Muslim Extremists will not be within a presidential term of office.

The enemy knows that U.S. public support or lack of support can change the operational tempo of war. America was pumped up while tanks screamed across the desert to oust Saddam at the beginning of the war, and the enemy tucked tail and ran. Conversely, Muqtada and the rest of the Muslim Extremists know that by producing a high body count, theirs or ours, at a particular time, when peace rallies or demonstrations are taking place, America acts divided and it helps their cause. Ample media coverage of peace rallies will even cause a president to react and slow things down to attempt to reduce the reported number of casualties, in order to maintain public support. A half-hearted commitment will not defeat this enemy or win this war.

The war against Muslim Extremists will continue long after the Iraqi Campaign has faded from the headlines and into the history books. Success will not come down to a series of pacifying tactical victories. Winning depends on whoever is most committed and has the most endurance for the strategic coup de grace.

This war must be fought from all sides, and public support is a side that can easily be exploited to their benefit or detriment. They see our compassion, kindness, and empathy as traits and opportunities that can be used against us. We won't kill them with kindness, and Hallmark doesn't make a card that can make them feel bad enough to stop. They also see our unity and motivation as something to be feared. We need the lasting commitment of our entire nation and to devote ourselves to finishing the job for as long as it takes.

The enemy has tried to kill me, and I have killed the enemy. My feeling about the whole situation is one of self-defense and necessity. I am a defender of my country's freedom, and it is my job to protect the gift of freedom for my people, and it is my job to stay alive for the ones I love back home. In this war, we all have the same job at home that Warfighters have on the battlefield, which is to protect freedom and to stay alive. America has taken nothing from Islam. Muslin Extremists like Muqtada al Sadr hate us for who we are, not what we have done.

Saddam killed Muqtada's father and brothers. Yet, even after America brought Saddam to justice, Muqtada didn't stop hating us. Muqtada would not exist if we had not removed Saddam. Many of us died while in the process of liberating Muqtada from Saddam, and he offered no appreciation. Instead, he slandered us and then he built an army to destroy the same people who sacrificed to save him. Defending ourselves against that kind of hatred will take the resolve of a unified country. It is better to have blood on our hands than it is to allow our lives to be taken. There is a time to kill.

Foreign Policy And Democracy

Chapter 18

Question: In what way has the American Army not done a good job in Iraq?

"They don't know how to satisfy the people. Even though the Americans are very smart, the British have more experience because Iraq was a British territory. Americans didn't have enough information and knowledge to deal with the Iraqi people. PsyOp has done the best job."

The one single voter in the United States who knows the most about foreign policy in Iraq is probably the Secretary of State, Condoleezza Rice. Currently, she has a horrible approval rating. She knows what needs to be done and she is doing her job as she was appointed to do by our elected president. From where I sit in Iraq, I would rather have this job and be fighting every day than take her place. Yes, I think that I could do her job, I think that I could do it well, and I wouldn't turn down the position if the president felt I was able to do it. Of course, that is a pipe dream; I don't have the educational background to even be considered. But let's try to understand for a minute and look at her situation, as if I was the secretary of state.

Here is what I would have to accomplish at a minimum: a foreign policy that would lead to success in Iraq without snubbing the Warfighters on the ground and their families, while at the same time appeasing the larger demographic of civilian voters who affect the president's approval rating. We have all heard the president say that he doesn't pay attention to approval ratings; horseshit! Politics are partially based on perception and opinions matter.

We live in a Democracy, so approval means a lot when it comes to votes, voters, and elections. Being successful as the secretary of state under these conditions is an impossible task because there is no way to make everyone happy. What do we do as a nation when the people of our Democracy do not agree with foreign policy and their approval conflicts with what may be best for our security? I think there's a lot of political sophomoric popularity vying that gets in the way of the serious security concerns of our foreign policy.

We have all learned that our government cannot always be trusted. Public trust and public faith have been scarred. Should we elect a new government to simply appease us? Then what happens if we are wrong? Will we as individual voters take the responsibility for the outcome?

If I was the secretary of state and did what the majority of the people wanted, but it was against my better judgment and our foreign policy failed, would you blame me or would you blame yourselves? At the same time, if you trusted me because our freely elected president appointed me and our foreign policy was successful, would you take the credit?

Now that I have seen what a world without a freely elected government is like and how its corruption is a cancer on an entire society, my views have changed. We all have opinions that are based upon our life experiences and education. I believe the war in Iraq was completely justified. I was also raised in a home where a picture of John Wayne hung over the kitchen table. My father is a former Marine and a Vietnam veteran, and my grandfather was also a former Marine who served during WWII in Japan, where he was a prisoner of war. Some would say that I have been indoctrinated as a Warfighter; as a child, yes. I believe that I was born a warrior then went to war and returned a poet. We all have different opinions, and our differences make us strong, or do they? Maybe only some of the time; no absolutes in my world.

I vote and make it a point to vote. My wife has never voted and she was raised very differently than I was. She never understood why I would throw a fit when people interrupted me when I watched a State of the Union address. She had never known anybody who served in a war other than her uncle, who served in Vietnam, and her family never seemed to hold much pride in that. I have heard her father say that he doesn't vote because he doesn't think it makes a difference, and her mom keeps her political beliefs "close to the vest."

This part is very hard for me to write about but I am going to say it because it makes my point. Since I have been in Iraq, my kids and wife have shed more tears than they probably ever will again, God willing. I say that because I have not made it home yet and there is still a fight outside that we ride into almost daily. These memories will shape them because they have sacrificed.

With all that said my wife cries to me over the phone and tells me she can't believe that she ever took her freedom for granted. One problem with this war is that so few people actually feel it, other than a news blurb and the "popular" monthly publicized body count. Other than being in the military, so few people actually participate and our military accomplishments are so rarely publicized. So many citizens participated in WWII and I think it made a difference, there was a sincere participation by everyone and that is a problem, today. My wife tells me that people just don't understand and that it sickens her to think she was the same way. She wrote a poem and is proud of it, and she should be. These are her words sent to me in a poem:

Sacrifice

A long, cold December night
I lie awake with tearand eyes
It's 2 a.m. I cannot sleep
Hours of worry flow through to my feet

I think about my husband gone
A brave young soldier for who I long
I remember when his arms of strong
Were wrapped around my body long

Taking away my pains and fears
Of everyday life that I sometimes drear
But now he's gone and I'm alone
Only memories of him when he was home

For now he is fighting to keep the peace
And help the Iraqis live their dreams
While U.S. protestors line our streets
Our military heroes feel their heat

Their job gets harder every day
My family suffers from the charades they play
The only wish for our kids this year
Is for Santa to bring back their daddy dear

For every time they see a plane
They think that Daddy is on his way
Only when his time has come
We will know his battle has been won

We all know we must be strong
And live our lives and carry on
Be proud, support our troops, and pray
That not one more life is lost today

For if it is and then I know
That hero gave me the freedoms I stow
I am grateful I am free

I don't take for granted simple grieves
I pray for safety, I pray for strength
I pray for the night I don't lie awake

A tearand eye will turn to joy
The minute I see my little boy
Grab Daddy's waist and hold him tight
And bring him home to bed at night.
Don't take life for granted ... support our
troops and their Mission!

Written: 12/12/05

My wife and I come from very different backgrounds. For now we are unified in our beliefs about sacrifice and freedom. She is looking forward to voting and she never misses a presidential speech. I don't think that our differences in America make us stronger on this issue, nor do I think the distrust and second-guessing of our government makes us stronger.

Less distrust and more citizen involvement makes sense if people really want change. Actually, I think distrusting a good government is just as detrimental as having a corrupt government, and unless we as a free and democratic people are willing to do all the research and take all the responsibility for our foreign policy, then we should all allow the people who know better to do their job. No different than the Warfighter on the ground, we should allow the people we elected to do their job with our confidence.

There is no way for our government to appeal to and appease all of us and still be effective. Life is full of pain and choices; surgery is painful ... but choosing surgery might save your life. Do you want the most popular doctor or the best doctor? Sometimes we act like paranoid cannibals and it does us no good.

Warfighters need to be able to do our job with the confidence of the American people, and politicians also need the same. Warfighters should not be politicians, and politicians should not be in the Warfighter business. As for those who are neither: Do your job as an American and make sure that you understand all the facts and take the individual responsibility to act as a Democratic people before you develop an opinion, cast a vote, or partake in a public demonstration that will affect foreign policy.

I am not advocating blind faith. I am just advocating ownership of personal actions that affect us all. Our choices make a difference. Our Declaration of Independence was written "for the people" and "by the people." Our forefathers risked everything and committed the crime of high treason with a penalty of death by simply discussing the writing of it. Individual responsibility came first in America before our freedom, and it will take the dependability of us all to maintain it. Like it or not, we are accountable to each other.

Our government is responsible to do what is in our best interest and that responsibility is reciprocal. We are responsible to do what is in our government's best interest for the survival of our Constitution and our future. If they don't protect our freedoms, then we have a duty to collectively remove them by force, if necessary. Foreign policy in Iraq is a "Catch-22" for a Democracy where people have become complacent with their responsibility and ownership of their actions because very few voters spend the time to weigh the long-term, secondary effects of pulling out too soon.

I rarely see the same fervor for a domestic issue that I have for a foreign issue, and there are more issues that challenge our freedom domestically at the municipal and state level than there are by any foreign policy. Truth be told, I trust my government more with foreign policy than I do domestic policy because all organisms protect themselves against foreign invaders. When my government does the same, I am protected, and as long as we don't sacrifice any of our sovereignty, this will be the case.

We are polarized to extremes by war. Every church-going soccer mom in America wanted revenge for the 9/11 attacks, and we got revenge. We decimated two countries because of an action that killed 2,800 Americans. Good for us! Will we allow our foreign advisors to the president to finish the job, now that we are not pissed off and simply want to kick somebody's ass?

War is a method to bring about change, and nothing more. When we look at war as only a method for revenge, then the change we seek does not have a chance to occur and we the people are to blame.

What does any of the information in this chapter have to do with our Tactical Psychological Operations Team, whispering truth from the shadows in Iraq? Foreign policy was influenced by "we the people" of our Democracy and affected our operations in Sadr City and our operations against Jaysh al Mehdi.

Straight From Team Voodoo: Nacho, Chesh, And Frank

Chapter 19

"All Information Is Good"

By: Sgt. Ed "Nacho" Kiedis

"Out of the Pan, Into the Fire"

By: Chesh (former Marine)

"It Worked ... So Thankful, I Got More Than I Banked On"

By: Sgt. Frank Rizzo (former Marine)

"All Information Is Good"

By: Sgt. Ed "Nacho" Kiedis

Tactical Psychological Operations Company (Airborne)

One night during a patrol, an insurgent tried to ambush the patrol and our team was involved in a shooting. We weren't all shooters but my team sergeant, Boone, was one of three shooters.

The other two shooters were soldiers from the platoon that we were out with that night. The entire situation from initial contact with the enemy to the enemy being KIA took about seven seconds, but the actual shooting took all of about three seconds in which our team sergeant fired three shots. After the man was down and the area was secured, I assessed the man to render medical aid. I checked for a pulse but none was found, and his pupils were fixed and dilated. I watched him as he exhaled his last breath and gurgled blood bubbles from his mouth.

Sometimes, the difference between them ambushing an unprepared patrol with automatic AK fire and killing us or the bad guy dying before he is able to kill, is what happens far in advance of leaving for the mission. Perhaps, as I tend to believe more and more, it is accomplished in all the years of preparation for such a mission and passed down from leaders to their subordinates. That is when a Warfighter learns to physically and mentally develop the ability to process the information that is being channeled to him at the speed of light and dissect the appropriate data. Success also comes in the aftermath by refining one's tactics and principles, which takes place when a mission is reviewed.

The patrol we were with that evening had been to this same location the night before but no one was seen on the grounds. What they found on the first night warranted another patrol being sent out for a second consecutive night. Our location that evening was in an area called Hababiya, which is a neighborhood on the southeast border of the notorious Sadr City, a literal haven for Muqtada's Militia, the Jaysh al Mehdi. Our team lived in Sadr City, so we could always spot the militia. We could "feel" them, being there (you would understand if you were there) when they were out for a public show of force whether or not they wore their canary-yellow shirts or dressed completely in black with a green bandana around their heads.

The location resembled something of a junkyard with several large metal conex containers situated on the grounds, with a white office trailer typical of what you might see on a construction site, where the superintendent might work. There were thousands of conspicuous open-ended, round metal tubes littered around the site and in piles around the entry to the site but hidden behind mounds of dirt. The piles were on either side of a short trail that led up to the white trailer and the location was hidden off of a main street in a dirt field about 200 meters out of view. Our vehicle was stopped on the dirt road that led to the location from the main road where we were conducting perimeter security, while Sgt. Cutler helped inspect the area. I was in charge of our security over-watch position for Sgt. Cutler and other soldiers as they made their way to the gate of the fence that surrounded the trailer.

There was nothing overtly suspicious about the location itself except for the conspicuous-looking metal tubes. They resembled what Haji likes to use for constructing improvised explosive devices that are placed on the side of the road to kill soldiers as they pass by in vehicles while on patrol. Usually the gunner and driver or TC [soldier in the passenger seat] get killed as the device detonates and metal propelled by explosive contents cuts through the armor of our Humvees and decapitates our gunners or takes his legs off, and the torso of the TC or driver receives the full measure of the blast. I was the team's driver so I had a vested interest in making sure that we caught the bad guys this evening. Because of what was here, the patrol on the night before had cut locks off some of the containers and gained entry to inspect several of them but some were left unopened and uninspected. That is why a second patrol was organized to return.

As the patrol and our team sergeant approached the gate that enclosed the trailer to make contact, they could see that a light was on inside. This night was different because a man was at the site. Haji had realized from the broken locks that the first patrol left behind that he needed to place a guard on the grounds to prevent anyone from gaining access and inspecting further. Though this was a smart thing to do on his part, what Haji didn't know was that we were part of the patrol this evening. For Haji, this information, or lack of it, was not good. The trailer sat approximately 30 meters behind a locked chain link fence, which was covered with black or green canvas that obscured the view of the trailer from anyone approaching from the outside, but the Haji inside could see us. A man was spotted inside the trailer but he was not armed at the time so our team sergeant made contact, giving a nonthreatening Arabic greeting, with his clearly American accent. The reason for a specific nonthreatening type of greeting is to try and make sure that an innocent "guard" would not become startled and make him a threat unknowingly. This was the technique we had used for approximately ten months and it never failed, except this Haji had us channeled between two metal containers and it was an ambush with ten of us in the kill zone. There was no place for us to go and only one way to stop this threat once he quickly grabbed his AK from the table that was out of view. It was time for all the years of training to pay off, because there ain't no second place in a gunfight.

The man seemed to hear the greeting but did not respond as they normally do, most guards are good people and simply are poor men that don't want any trouble, so the interpreter was used to tell the man to open the door to the trailer and come out. Through the canvass fence, our team sergeant, prepared to take action, was observing the man's actions through a small hole in the canvas just large enough to get a site picture with his weapon. At this point, the man was facing our direction towards the fence where our team sergeant called out to him from, and he stood at an open window looking outward as if to acknowledge the voices coming from the soldiers outside.

His posture was not threatening nor was it passive. He simply looked indifferent and this was unusual. He crossed his arms and paused for a second but still did not comply, something wasn't "right" simply by the "way" he turned. Then he turned suddenly, facing his back to the open window, picked up his AK, and turned to face the open window once more. When he began to raise his rifle, shots were fired, and the bad guy was down.

After the shooting, the soldiers had to remove the gate from the hinges because it was locked from the inside. Our team sergeant and other soldiers made their way up to the trailer. When the scene was being assessed for further information, our team sergeant (Boone) was quick to ascertain that two of his shots had hit the man in the chest, and one of his shots missed to the left and hit the exterior of the trailer that the man stood in as he held an AK-47 with two taped-together magazines inserted in the magazine well of his weapon. I spoke with Boone at a later date about the shooting and he described the chain of events to me as they took place in his mind. Despite a common belief that these types of events are traumatizing and leave emotional and psychological scars behind, Boone relayed to me that the entire event unfolded before him in a series of small "packets" of information chained together, which he used to validate the man's actions, and he used each "packet" of information to initiate his response in accordance with the threat level. In military terms, this is called escalation of force.

For Boone, it was all about acquiring the threat by getting a good site picture, followed by two accelerated shots, and then an additional site picture for a follow-up shot until the threat was eliminated. The whole incident went down in his mind just as thousands of other training scenarios that had taken place over years as not only a military firearms instructor but a civilian firearms instructor. The whole event came down to a series of decisions Boone made, not simply one decision. These were also techniques that he had taught our entire team during several opportunities. The enemy showed, by his actions, that he had hostile intent and was, in fact, moving to the next level of trying to take American lives. We all had to learn, if you know what to look for, it is fairly easy to identify and articulate why you believe someone is trying to kill you long before you actually see bullets coming your way, and why you should respond with deadly force.

So after the shooting, when Boone moved forward to secure the area, he then confirmed his shots, whether good or bad. He identified two hits and one miss. The whole thing was just like a training event and came down to conditioned responses instilled through thousands of training cycles with the exception that one bad guy was dead and out of the terrorism business. U.S.: one, terrorists: zero, at least for the evening.

One could argue that a man lying in wait to kill you, facing you head-on with a fully loaded AK-47, and raising his muzzle to unload on your ass is bad information! The same could be said of the shot that Boone fired and missed. What if the rounds that had penetrated the bad guy had not been enough to kill the man before he engaged with his weapon and sprayed the courtyard that was full of soldiers that night? At least seven soldiers were in the bad guy's line of fire when he was killed. Again, you could say that this is bad information your brain is feeding you via your optical nerves. In fact, the bad guy did get one shot off but it was believed that he squeezed the trigger on his way down after being shot several times, and none of our guys were hurt.

However, on the other hand, there exists another discipline of thought among those who have paid the cost through thousands of proper training cycles under the tutelage of experienced instructors, who themselves possess this discipline. I am not talking about some mysterious ancient Ninja tactic that only a few initiated know. The discipline boils down to this: One has to have put in the hours of principle-based training and therefore have enough of a base of knowledge to review whatever just took place from a constructively critical point of view, so that learning can take place and improvements can be made.

This makes all information useful whether it confirms or denies the effectiveness of your course of action. For those who have these vital skills in a combat zone, each mission is an opportunity to learn from and become an expert Warfighter. Each new segment of data, whether it poses a threat or enhances the mission, is fuel that propels the combustion of the mind and is accessed to facilitate skills and resources, so that the mission may be accomplished successfully.

Our goal is to move through each event, without hesitation, in a given timeline, while acting with intent and in complete open consciousness. Therefore, for the experienced Warfighter, all information is good. This may seem elementary. I cannot tell you how many missions our team went on where mistakes were made and our team made the difference between the success and failure of the mission because we were able to mentally process and relay more information. Though it may sound like I am tooting our own horns, in fact, all I am saying is that we had more knowledge and confidence to move through certain situations without hesitation.

To clarify, there is a process in the U.S. Army for reviewing an individual's or a unit's actions to improve all aspects of performance. This process is called an After Action Review or AAR. An AAR should be performed after every mission for the purpose of honestly assessing the situation and to seek improvement.

However, there is a difference between effectively and honestly conducting an AAR and taking a slipshod jab at one. Many leaders will attempt to conduct AARs but will fail to do it effectively because they do not have the basic knowledge that is required to critique the mission properly. As a result, the good process of improving on performance is turned into a required task instead of how it was designed. Therefore, the principle derived from the process meant to make improvements is no longer applied, thus rendering the review useless. This becomes the model for younger soldiers to imitate, and a bad habit is born and perpetuated. If someone does not have the principle-based knowledge they need to navigate through extreme situations, they will repeat mistakes while continuing to move through the event. Or even worse, they will nut up, and rather than accomplish the mission, they will circumvent the challenge or halt completely.

You would think these individuals would review the mission in hopes of learning how to correct their mistakes. However, it has been my experience that they will often pat themselves on the back for a mission well accomplished despite the glaring errors that were made; of course these are not the actions of all but many. For this individual, all information is not seen as being good, and it is easier to ignore the truth than to deal with the possibility of owning up to his or her mistakes. All information isn't good to these individuals because they either don't possess the humility and hunger to learn, or they do not feel they have the knowledge base or leadership above them to submit their actions for healthy scrutiny from which they can grow as soldiers, they become hesitant about the truth or worried about being reprimanded for mistakes, and sometimes a leader's mistakes follow them, so what are their real choices? If a scenario, or some form of it, has not been seen enough times, lack of training and the absence of conditioned responses will breed hesitation when faced with having to process new information, while controlling their emotions if information from these events is perceived as negative. If someone in a leadership role reaches this point of critical mass, it will cause the entire patrol to hesitate at a critical juncture until someone comes along and gets it moving again. If lower enlisted soldiers reach this point without proper leadership and mentoring, they will learn to handle different situations without the proper principles and continue in their careers as soldiers with bad habits. As a result, you get soldiers hanging their hats on actions that were badly executed and sticking a feather in their caps for less-than-noteworthy combat performance.

Whether a unit is involved in full-scale kinetic operations or a battalion commander is involved in extended battle focused non-kinetic dialogue with a terrorist faction representative, the combat zone is a cheese grater. A soldier's skills, wits, and efforts are pressed against the blade on one side, and out from the other side, the honest truth of his ability is distilled for everyone to witness. Mistakes will be made, but without confidence and an environment that promotes learning from one's own mistakes, those mistakes will be incorrectly assessed and the proper adjustments will not be made. Too many leaders get reprimanded for acting and making mistakes that cause them to not want to share their mistakes. Thus, learning ceases and mistakes are slid under the radar. Therefore, soldiers become dishonest about their mistakes and abilities. These are perhaps at the cost of their lives or the lives of other soldiers, or at the cost of losing a war only to have to fight it again. You might be lucky for a while, and I guess luck is a good thing. However, "I'd rather be good than lucky because luck runs out."

Airborne!

"Out of the Pan, Into the Fire"
By: Chesh (Former Marine)
Tactical Psychological Operations Company (Airborne)

I transferred to Team Voodoo later in our deployment and from the first moment, I knew I was going to see and do some of the world's best PsyOp. Not only was I going to get to learn, see, and do some great things but I was going into the heart of the war in Iraq, Sadr City. The one place that can send shivers down people's spine at the mere mentioning of its name. I have to be honest, after being in Iraq for six months before they unexpectedly moved me to Sadr City; however, it was somewhat expected at the same time. I believed in my heart that the Areas of Operations (AOs) I had been in were not challenging enough for me. I felt loyal to my old team and moving from one team to another was a surprise, yet moving to Sadr City was not. I had heard all the horror stories of Sadr City

181

and read some books on it, so I felt that I was finally ready to make my acquaintance.

I really didn't know the guys of 1412 except from a couple of brief introductions at detachment meetings, by my previous team sergeant, SFC Byrd. He told me that if I was to be removed from his team to go anywhere that he was glad for me to be part of Boone's team. So, I went with an open mind about all the new things I would have a chance to learn and all the different things I would see. I will never forget the drive from my old Forward Observation Base Falcon to my new one, FOB Hope, as we drove through Sadr City. All the Local Nationals, and I truly mean ALL, in the city looked at our American convoy like they were all ready to grab their weapons and light us up. I remember waving at people as we drove by to get a feel for how the people interacted with the Americans. I finally got one little boy to smile and wave back. As I sighed with some feeling of humanity, his father was there beside him and pushed him inside their courtyard, clearly disappointed at his son for showing such a minute form of kindness towards us.

My time with Voodoo in Sadr City was short lived because at the end of 2005 the powers that be decided to give the Sadr City Area of Operations to the fledgling, corrupted Iraqi Army and close down FOB Hope. Myself and the team were still fairly new at working together when we were reassigned to FOB Rustamyhia to support a new unit. The new unit arrived in country was the 3rd Battalion, 67th Armored Regiment, 4th Infantry Division attached to the 101st Airborne Division. Some of the unit's soldiers were on their second tour, but most of them were new and didn't have any warfighting experience. So, as the subject matter experts in the Area of Operation, it was our job to help the new unit until they gained some experience and understanding of what's going on in Iraq at that time in their area.

The transition from 3rd Infantry Division to 4th Infantry Division was a lot harder than I had initially anticipated. A good majority of the new guys were jacked up, so not only did we have to advise them from the psychological aspect, but also we had to teach them how to operate in Iraq on a combat patrol. The first few weeks of working with our new supported unit was real interesting. Platoons that I thought were really jacked up quickly turned things around and later impressed me with their eagerness to learn about how to function on patrol and how to interact with the people of Iraq. Unfortunately, there was also a flipside to that coin and some platoons progressively got worse as time went on. I can honestly say that if it weren't for the platoons that made a quick adjustment to the new environment and culture shock, I would have more than likely given up on them. I would have been more than content with trying to convince my team sergeant to say, "Screw them" and "find" other missions.

By this point, I felt completely comfortable with my new brethren of Voodoo and also felt integrated throughout every aspect of the team. I was learning new things and was able to apply them effectively. I had already learned on every mission, every day. My team sergeant, Sgt. Cutler, challenged me in every aspect of my job and in every aspect of being a better soldier. At first, I was "in awe" over what I would see every day on missions with Boone, and by the time the new unit came in I was also doing things in ways that produced results every time we entered the arena. This was the reason my old team sergeant accepted me being moved. I appreciate him knowing what was best for my development and even though he needed me, he supported my transfer to Sgt. Boone Cutler's team.

Needless to say, I could not have been happier with my new family. I had been in the military for a while now and this was the first time I was on a team that everyone knew their job and did it without anyone telling them what to do and how to do it. I believe our age had something to do with it. I am the youngest at twenty-seven so the maturity level was not ever in question; rank really didn't need to exist. We were able to function as a well-oiled machine. Because we worked on everything we did together so often, we always knew what the other guy was thinking but more importantly, what he was about to do. We had a saying on the team; Boone used to say that there are only three things you need to do to be successful: "Anticipate, anticipate, anticipate." That is what we did and it eliminated complacency.

One of the many times we went out on patrol and had to do some teaching with a good patrol leader was with B Company. The PL was a great student of war and is very quick on the uptake. Our team needed to revisit a house in their area near Tissa Nissan, generally quiet, so after coordinating with them we rolled out to our destination. When we reached the house we were immediately scolded for being late, but right after, it was hugs all around. The family had lived in Iraq all their lives and the man of the household served with the British during WWII. He was a person who I could just listen to for hours. The family invited us into a large family room that was very well furnished. There were quite a few people. I decided since I had already been here before and had a chance to chat with this family that I would sit away from the crowd. My quick-study PL was already advised not to interfere until he was introduced; also, this was a great time to whisper in his ear and school him about what was taking place.

Boone spearheaded the conversation to accomplish our mission that night. The PL sat down beside me out of the obtrusive view. He and I were the only two sitting outside of conversation distance from the family, but we were still within range to hear everything that was said. The PL was very interested in what was going on, I explained what was being said and, more importantly, why. Boone wasn't just talking, he was working, and every word or sentence had a direction and reason. It was more like a psychological dance or play, and Boone did things that were unseen but very important. So, I told the PL how this "play" was working. I continued to tell him *how* Boone was going about discussing the important topic and key words he was using to make the family feel or do specific things depending on what it was we needed to accomplish.

Empowerment was a big thing we worked on, and I guess you could say it is equivalent to a coach's big pregame speech. It opens up in a systematic way of dragging information out of people and leaves them with changed emotions. I explained every word that Boone was saying to the family and what he was about to say next. I also pointed out that Boone was doing other things to increase his effectiveness like using the tone of his voice to help convey his message. Boone's body language was also a big part of it, I explained to the PL. At that time, we still had our great interpreter before he returned home to the States. He worked with us so much and was on the same page that his tone changed with Boone's tone and his body language did the same. After a while, I began explaining other things that we did like growing long hair and thick mustaches. These were some of the important things that were typically seen as out of regulation and undisciplined. While the Army frowned upon them, these things got us in and out of places we would have never been able to go.

The PL was so impressed that after the mission he wanted to change jobs and do what our team does, which isn't uncommon for people who understand. A few weeks after that mission, I saw him growing his hair out and letting his mustache grow in. Unfortunately, we knew that he was not going to be able to continue that because "Big Army" doesn't allow soldiers to think and act for themselves. "Big Army" is designed to be in control all the time. That's what should make a Special Operations unit different from the rest of the Army. We don't have to be in control all the time, just when and only when it truly matters. The vehicle was always ready, gear always prepped, food, water, etc.

Being a team was the easy part and allowed us to focus on what we needed to focus on, which was the enemy. The enemy was and is ever-changing, and we must be ever-changing as well. So, we did that and continued to up until we left the Sand Box. What a great team we were. Boone, Nacho, Frank, and me . . . we really did have the corner on the market in Sadr City and then for a short time in the Tissa Nissan AO.

"It Worked . . . So Thankful, I Got More Than I Banked On"
By: Sgt. Frank Rizzo (Former Marine)
Tactical Psychological Operations Company (Airborne)

For the record, I just want to say that by no means was I nor am I a PsyOp guru. When I showed up on the team, I was a skill level 1 PsyOp'er, an E-5/Sgt. And that is not good for the rank I held! Boone took the time, was patient, and taught me by the numbers what was going on, from basic tasks to advanced PsyOp skills. He got me up to speed and integrated me into the team, and I fell into the rhythm of what was going on. Boone was a leader to us all, too bad his self-taught brilliance went unnoticed, tragic actually.

Looking back, I am impressed with his interpersonal skills. He is a master of communication with everyone from the lowliest private on up to the battalion commander or even a demoralized group of legitimately honest Iraqi Army soldiers, and they would all not just hear but respond. After speaking to some demoralized IA, they got motivated and went toe-to-toe with some Mahdi Militia and took them on in a firefight a week later, all because he, through an interpreter, "empowered" them. You would have to see it to believe it, he could have a one-on-one conversation connection with a group of people. That was real PsyOp and would blow my mind. The rest of the team and I would try to figure out how he did it with such apparent ease. He just did it "right" and produced actual results that went unnoticed by our command. He should be a teacher of non-kinetic operations for the entire military to create continuity that we need because that is a real problem. Just listening to him is like sitting in a room with Freud and Thomas Edison, I can't explain his techniques and he would never let me try because of his Operational Security concerns that are always at the top of his list.

I think PsyOp would be more effective if everyone was on the same page. It seemed like everyone felt free to interpret PsyOp doctrine as they saw fit. I worked for another TPT whose team sergeant claimed he was a cultural expert on Baghdad but whose sole purpose in life was to ensure we did our part to make sure product was distributed (paperboys in essence) in a timely fashion so we could make room for the next batch of newspapers, soccer balls, key chains, T-shirts, etc. on our weekly/biweekly detachment product-runs to FOB Victory. "Never mind supporting the battalion, let's get back and play video games" seemed to be our goal. However, to be fair product distribution "by doctrine" is a huge part of the way the PsyOp techniques are taught at the schoolhouse, so I can't pick on them too much but I didn't see the same effectiveness as what Boone did with words. The other team "checked the block" but I don't think they accomplished the PsyOp mission to influence attitudes and change behavior.

In closing, I would like to say this is just an example of one team's effort that affects change. I would like to see an entire whole PsyOp taskforce using Boone's techniques to get his results across the theater; the face of the war could be very different today, I have little doubt this would be absolutely true. Not trying to downplay everyone else, I'm sure everyone had their own brand of success and most tried their best; they just didn't know better. This is just one man's lowly opinion. I can't finish without saying; the time I spent with Voodoo not only made me a better skilled "Tactical" PsyOp'er and took me from my less than appropriately skilled level to the skill level I should have already known. Boone never humiliated me or ignored my shortcomings, he encouraged me and simply made it happen as a true leader; he was never too busy to teach. Additionally, this may seem out of place but Sgt. Cutler taught me valuable tools for life after the war and throughout my life. I am very grateful to him. Sorry, if I got off theme, I ain't a writer, but this really is deserved and needed to be said. And, I haven't even told you about the tricks he taught us that brought us all home.

Turps

Chapter 20

This chapter is dedicated to an interpreter named "Chicago." He knew the price of freedom and ended up being murdered for helping Americans bring democracy to Iraq.

We had a few interpreters in Iraq. They all have code names that we used for them in sector because they are always in danger of being killed for working with Americans. Interpreters are generally a good cross section of the populace of Iraq and have been very helpful to our team by teaching us their cultural knowledge. Some are very good and some are not so good. Some are very honest and some are spies, but generally, they bridge the communication gap between the Iraqi people and us. I wanted to finish this book by showing you that these ideas, from page 1 to now . . . come mainly from the Iraqi people that I learned from. This should solidify the information that you have learned. People that have read advanced copies of the book, report that they now understand the news and can pick apart the bullshit from the reality. I will say again and I truly believe this, I do not blame the media for inconsistencies or wrong info because they simply don't have the resources, access, and techniques to get what I have shared with you.

Our interpreters live in constant fear and many have been killed. Oftentimes, their entire families are threatened. They spend so much time with us that they actually become members of the team. They get kudos like other team members and they get chewed out just as any other members, and without them we couldn't do our job. Just like us, they get moody, are sometimes lazy, but they get motivated and inspired by the work. They take orders from us and sometimes they don't like it, but they drive on just like a soldier. Together we work through conflicts with each other. In every way, other than wearing "U.S. Army" on their uniform, our "turps" are members of the team and they see it all with us.

As we end our combat tours in Iraq, the interpreters are the ones who stay behind and get turned over and passed on to incoming teams. They are not equipment and they deserve the utmost respect from the American soldiers and the American people. I have probably been shot at with my interpreter present more than I have with any single member of my team or any other American. I even allow our turps to carry weapons when most units don't, but don't tell anyone because I am not supposed to.

They never leave but we rotate in and out of the war. They are patriots of Iraq and many have given their lives to save their country. We have tried to help our interpreters find ways to immigrate to America but their options are nearly impossible and their immigration opportunities to other Coalition-backed countries are very limited;

I completely disagree with that. Others get U.S. immunity in the States but why not them . . . they have earned it in my view. I asked one of our interpreters a few questions and his answers are annotated below. None of these statements are more than his opinion. This is a great opportunity for us all to see how an Iraqi citizen sees the world in Iraq. These are his answers EXACTLY verbatim and without any prompting, other than giving him precise directions to be completely honest. When we were finished with each question, I asked him if I wrote exactly what he wanted to say. All of the words here are his. I asked him to speak freely and honestly from his heart. I can say that his sentiment is very consistent with that of other Iraqi friends that I have spoken with. Some of his honesty did surprise me and I am proud of his forthcoming candor.

I hope this conversation "sticks" with you because this maybe the only opportunity for you all to hear candid conversation from an Iraqi man raised Muslim in an Arab country that was unfriendly to America. This is the conversation that you have seen in parts throughout the book and the complete context is very powerful.

Interpreters often had to hide their faces and identities from each other in order to stay safe.

This is some of the most important information that Americans can know and learn. From person to person, and with politics aside from the human perspective, here is what they have to say and what they feel.

Question: How were you raised to feel about Americans?

Answer:

We were raised to feel Americans were the biggest enemy to Islam and we must stop them from doing what they want against Islam. We were taught to fight them in order to stop them from hurting Islam. We were taught to fight them by any means necessary. For instance, we were taught to stop buying their stuff since the Americans were not in Iraq at that time. We were taught to fight them even in the smallest ways. Saddam and his regime enhanced this because he also hated America. We were taught special lessons in school and made to repeat slogans and chants that were anti-American. The chants also included glorifying Islam, Saddam, and the homeland. I can't remember the exact words right now but I do remember many lessons and slogans being taught to me since I was very young. All my family was the same way.

Question: Why did you become an interpreter?

Answer:

I like English and I felt that I was able to communicate with soldiers. It was an adventure for me at first because I was meeting new people and helping them to save my people. At that time, I didn't have to wear a mask or disguise. I liked helping Americans communicate with the people. It was a good way for me to get help for my people and I liked the money. My main reason is because I was exploring a new thing and helping my country. I absolutely enjoyed it in the beginning. It was the best thing that I ever did until it became dangerous.

Question: How is PsyOp different from other Army units?

Answer:

PsyOp has specific goals, and they try to understand the people and understand the way that we think. They look for opinions and the work they do is not for a short period of time, but they look for long-term solutions. They try to figure out the general atmospheric information of the people's attitudes in the area, and by doing this, it helps solve problems for the people. I have worked for four PsyOp teams and they were all different; some I liked more than others. Sgt. Cutler's team is the fourth team that I have worked for.

The first team I worked with had two main concerns and they were concerned with helping the people and determining what the political parties were trying to do. Some of the political parties were trying to find jobs and others were trying to find opportunities to keep young people from becoming thieves. For example, we had a good relationship with the Da'awa Party and they turned in weapons to us. That first team helped old Ba'ath Party members take a new oath to support the new Iraq. As a result, we got many weapons out of the hands of people that could have become used by insurgents.

The second team came in on the 28th of February 2004 and the first uprising in Sadr City started shortly after. They tried to continue what the first team started and met with leaders of the political parties regularly. The political parties were trying to get help to rebuild Sadr City and had plans for projects. We helped them secure their headquarters building, by building walls and providing weapons permits to their guards. In return, we got Intelligence information against ex-Ba'ath Party members and the Fadaeen. We were able to facilitate services in exchange for helping with the security situation and they gave us Intelligence Information. At that time, the Sadr Bureau was not part of helping the situation in Sadr City. However, they were willing to consider being helpful to us at the time.

On the day we had a meeting with them, we went to the Sadr Bureau, but a member of the Sadr Bureau, Sheikh Hazeem al Araji, met us there before we went inside. He said that the meeting was cancelled because Paul Bremmer had shut down the production of the *Al Houza* newspaper. The Sadr Bureau produced this newspaper. Because of this, the Sadr Bureau was no longer willing to be part of the reconstruction effort for Sadr City, and it was also the start of the bad relationship between the Americans and the Sadr Bureau.

Soon after the first uprising in Sadr City started, the second team I was with could not leave the FOB much and was very restricted. Their efforts and the progress vanished. At times, we went out with patrols that we thought would not be shot at and attempted to convince them to stop the fighting. In return, the Sadr followers responded to us by showing us their hatred. From that time, I had to start living on the FOB and I had to wear a mask and body armor. It was the start of a very dangerous time. We even had to stay at another location to launch patrols because the routes coming out of the FOB were too dangerous. Other times, we had to patrol in Bradley Fighting Vehicles instead of our Humvees.

One day, the battalion commander's interpreter was not available, so I went with the battalion commander, Lieutenant Colonel Volesky from 2/5 Cav, to the al Jazaair Iraqi Police Station. We met with members of the Sadr Bureau. I remember Saed Kareem al Bukhati being there and doing a lot of the talking. I went with him to attempt to negotiate a peace settlement between Jaysh al Mehdi and the Americans. We told them that Jaysh al Mehdi must give up their weapons. The Iraqi Police would be responsible for the internal security of Sadr City and the Iraqi Army would be responsible for the perimeter security. I really liked Lieutenant Colonel Volesky because he told the Sadr Bureau that the Americans were willing to keep fighting but if they wanted to help their people, then it was up to them to make the changes. He had a very strong character and I admired him. The Sadr Bureau listened to him but they had some conditions. However, in the second meeting, he made them drop their conditions in order to achieve the peace settlement.

The third team that I worked with got here when it was peaceful. They helped with crowd control situations at a propane station.

They were very good with the people and they made the people feel comfortable. They were very effective at learning what was going on. Sometimes, they could be violent when it was necessary, but they were good. They worked very well as a team and they took turns running the missions. I liked working with them the most. We joked a lot and we had a lot in common, and we were all the about the same age. When we went on missions, I really liked it and bugged them if we didn't go out. Oftentimes, I stayed with them in their living area instead of mine. They also had a good relationship with each other. They were not the best at PsyOp but they were a good team for each other and myself.

The current team, with Sgt. Cutler, is always trying to be creative and analyze the situation. We always try to find solutions for any kind of problem and constantly make contacts with the many Iraqi people. We are good at listening to the people and telling them why we are here and what can be done to make the situation better. We negotiate constantly by telling them what they can do for us and what we can do for them. We would do better if the supported unit would allow us more accessibility to more people.

Much of the time, we educated the people to participate in the elections and freely select a candidate without being afraid. We taught the people the true meaning of Democracy and they reacted positively. Sgt. Cutler and I have been shot at a lot together, and we respond by finding different ways to stop the violence before it happens. Sgt. Cutler is the most serious team sergeant that I have had. He is the most focused. The first team sergeant I had tried to be like Sgt. Cutler but he couldn't because he was a beginner.

Question: What ways do you hide yourself to keep yourself safe?

Answer:

I always have to hide myself to be safe. I met a new interpreter one time and tried to tell him what to do and he didn't listen to me, and he was killed the day after I met him. If I go out, I don't take the same routes and I always try to blend in with other Iraqis. I hide any U.S. equipment or documents. I don't wear the same things that I wear on missions. Right now, there are many Jaysh al Mehdi checkpoints and one of the things they look for are interpreters that work for Americans. Realistically, they probably already know who I am since I worked at FOB Hope. I know that there is probably an interpreter that I know that works for Jaysh al Mehdi. When my friends ask me to pose for a photo, I won't do it because I don't want them to have an easy time getting a picture of me. Most of the time, I live on the FOB and I always wear a mask when I go out on a mission with the team. The road to my home is very dangerous to travel.

Question: How difficult has being an interpreter made your life?

Answer:

In the beginning as an interpreter, my life was so perfect. I was doing the job that I liked to do, I made enough money to get what I want, I helped my family, and I was helping the people of my country. I really loved helping my people. I made $300 per month and that was about 600,000 Iraqi dinar. Then everything collapsed and it became chaos in my life. Instead of being safe and going home and not worrying about people killing me, I had to always look over my shoulder. Now I make $1,050 per month and that is about 1.5 million Iraqi dinar. The economy has gotten much better since the Americans came. They have paid me fairly by raising my salary to adjust for the cost of living. My close family knows that I am an interpreter and they ask to borrow money from me. I cannot tell anybody that I am an interpreter because I will be killed.

My hardest part to deal with is that I have lost my friends. I used to have a lot of friends but now I cannot see them anymore because it is not safe for me to go meet with them. We used to go together to smoke the Hooka pipe and hang out. We used to go to the arcade and stay a long time playing games, joke around, and just have fun. I have a lot of friends. Now, the only thing I do is go on missions and I spend time at the Internet café on the FOB where I can safely chat with people and meet them. Seeing my family is usually very tense and I cannot stay for long, usually only about fifteen minutes or so, just long enough to drink some tea. Six of my friends that were interpreters have been killed. I would like to leave Iraq because things are getting worse everyday.

Question: How have you seen PsyOp teach the people in Iraq about Democracy?

Answer:

We told the people that they have the power to fix the problems by voting for the right person. If someone was not properly representing them then they have the right to vote them out of office. Voting and selecting representatives was their constitutional right. Sgt. Cutler used different speeches that were tailored for different people and situations. For instance, if people had a problem getting help and the DAC members were not helping them, then they could vote for new DAC members that would be helpful. I have seen Sgt. Cutler use approximately thirty different speeches to teach people about Democracy.

Question: How have you helped American soldiers?

Answer:

I helped soldiers by educating them on my culture and how not to take the wrong ways that make things worse or more difficult.

Question: How do you feel when you see American soldiers kill Iraqis?

Answer:

I feel so bad. I wish that this thing never happened and I imagine myself in their place because I am one of them. It makes it worse when they get killed for stupid reasons that didn't make sense. I have been angry with Americans when they killed Iraqis unless they are killed when they were trying to hurt me and the Americans I am with. I am not mad at Americans for killing Iraqis while trying to protect themselves, but during the uprising in Sadr City, some Iraqis were innocent and in the line of fire so they were killed accidentally. I remember some Iraqi soldiers that were accidentally killed by Americans and it honestly made me mad. It is true that it was an accident but good soldiers should not do such a thing.

Question: What is the best thing you have seen the current team do?

Answer:

They educated the people on the street and explained to them that they had rights under a Democracy. This team inspired people to stand up and resist the Jaysh al Mehdi Punishment Committee. The people who were Sadr followers understood about what the Punishment Committee did but they began to speak against Jaysh al Mehdi, and the people that were not Sadr followers changed their minds and rejected the tactics of the Punishment Committee. This was a very good thing, courage.

Question: What do you like most about the Americans that you work with?

Answer:

I like the way they work and follow through on what they say they will do. They try very hard to do things the way they should be done. They are very educated and have knowledge about many things. They have taught me many things for me to become better. Working with them is like reading a book.

Question: In what way has the American Army not done a good job in Iraq?

Answer:

They don't know how to satisfy the people. Even though the Americans are very smart, the British have more experience because Iraq was a British territory. Americans didn't have enough information and knowledge to deal with the Iraqi people. PsyOp has done the best job.

Question: What is the best thing that the American Army did for Iraq?

Answer:

Getting rid of Saddam was the best thing and the worst thing because they were not prepared to finish the job. When the Americans first got here, they did not protect the Iraqi Ministries and infrastructure. That was the first thing that it has made it hard and difficult to get Iraq back on its feet. The Americans did not protect the old Iraqi Army camps, and a lot of weapons fell into the hands of the insurgents. That was the first place that the insurgency got their weapons to fight Americans. Jaysh al Mehdi, Ansar al Sunna, and other groups used these weapons to fight American soldiers, and since then it has been more difficult. Iraq had approximately 500,000 soldiers plus another 750,000-member "popular" army that was run by the Ba'ath Party members.

The "popular" army soldiers were like Reserve soldiers and many of them could be forced to fight in times of need. There were enough weapons for all of them, and we had a lot of weapons. We had factories that made weapons. My brothers told me about all these Iraqi Army camps that were looted, and they remember discussing how it was a big deal at the time.

Question: Did America win or lose the war in Iraq?

Answer:

America won because they achieved their goal. They got rid of Saddam and established a government that is represented by the people.

Question: What should America do to Muqtada al Sadr and Jaysh al Mehdi?

Answer:

Let the government deal with them. That will give the government confidence in themselves. If they do a good job, then it means that it can run itself. I want Jaysh al Mehdi to be split up, and if possible, they can get jobs with Iraqi Security Forces, but only if they are willing to serve the government and not the religious leaders.

Question: If Jaysh al Mehdi is not split up, do you think they can destroy the government?

Answer:

Yes, they could destroy the government. But they won't because right now they control most of the government and they won't destroy themselves.

Conclusion

"I know not what course others may take; but for me, give me liberty or give me death!" are words of Patrick Henry spoken on March 23, 1775. The speech was given without notes, it was inspiring, and Americans felt so empowered that they agreed to take part in what lead to our Revolutionary War. Voodoo in Sadr City tried the same thing and empowered the people of Iraq through mentoring and teaching the value of Democracy—it worked for a time, until we got pulled out. It could work again.

The word "Liberty" can be defined as the state of being free within a society from oppressive restrictions imposed by authority on one's way of life, or political views—the power or scope to act as one pleases.

That's me with no mustache and a hangover with my dad. I talk a lot of trash about Marines but keep in mind that half of Voodoo are former Marines and I have nothing against those Warfighters, I do it in COMPLETE jest. (For the Marines, that means I'm joking—Sounds like "Joe King.") I only do it because joining the Army and being the son of a career Marine left me open to a lot of trash talking myself, I am just trying to keep up. If more Marines were Paratroopers maybe I would have joined the Marines but not even a Marine is a substitute for a Paratrooper. Relax Jarheads, it was just another joke.

Today is September 2, 2007, it's my birthday and my dad is here with me at Walter Reed to visit. He arrived a few days ago; we haven't seen each other in about ten years or so. My mom sent him to visit as a birthday gift to us both; it's a guy thing because we wouldn't have done it for each other: that's what phones are for. The last time we saw each other was at my grandfather's funeral. I don't know all the reasons he decided to come here now other than my birthday and maybe I don't need to know.

I know that since he has been here we have had a few drinks together, watched a ball game, visited the DC memorials and even got tattooed together ... hey, that's a definite guy thing. It was my dad's first tattoo and he's sixty years old. For a former Marine I guess he took it pretty good—at least until Mom sees it. (Sorry Dad, I couldn't resist that one.)

I've been to the place where the tough guys go and come out on the other side—Sadr City. Since I've been back, I have been through my own brand of mass confusion. I've lost my second marriage as of late, lived through the Walter Reed "scandal" and all after getting busted up in Iraq and still finishing my tour. Starship Reed got me hooked on dope twice (not like I wasn't willing to "go there"—pain hurts! I just didn't know where it was ending up while being isolated and locked away) ... But hey, shit happens and I ain't the only Warfighter that shit happens to. I'm just scratching the surface so wait for the next book—just in case I decide to put myself through this torture again because shit is happening to a lot of Warfighters, believe me!

While walking I looked at the war memorials around DC with my dad. He said that he wondered what type of memorial they might make for GWOT, Global War on Terror, veterans from Iraq and Afghanistan. The issue seemed strange to me. War memorials are supposed to be something held in esteem and I'm not sure if my country supports us winning or even participating in this war. I hear people say that they support the troops but not the war and I'm sorry to say but that feels a little back-handed. Like, someone saying, "Black people are great but supporting the Civil Rights movement just isn't my thing." There is no way around it though and it's okay for us to disagree. We all subscribe to our own brand of ignorance. That's what part of freedom is all about so I'm just telling it as plainly as I can so me and Warfighters with the same perspective can be heard. I appreciate those people for being generally kind and I think most don't understand because the mission is poorly explained to the American public. Hopefully, *Voodoo in Sadr City* will bring some clarity.

What are they really disagreeing with . . . The fact war exists? Going to war in the first place? The fact that people die? I suspect that if the war had been over in three weeks, gas prices had gone down, and it wasn't a daily factor on the news, most of them wouldn't even have ever taken the time to develop an opinion nor do they really understand the one they have now. They are today's version of the antiwar protestor. It's all done in a subdued politically correct method since they don't want the negative public stigma from the 1960s or 70s pop-culture. But, if that is as close as we get to draft dodging, riots, and massive flag burning in the street then I guess I'd say that we have something as a nation to be proud of.

Jokingly, I told my dad that the GWOT War Memorial would probably be a big middle finger sticking out of the ground. He laughed and said that he thought the same after returning from Vietnam back in '69. No doubt Vietnam vets were seemingly hated when they returned, and there was no excuse for it other than ignorance. That time in our history is so much more than tragic and embarrassing. Many of those same Warfighters that got spit on when they returned are quietly making sure that we are getting taken care of now. I've heard some incredible stories at the hospital.

Vietnam vets were known for being openly disrespected. In this generation, the Iraq and Afghanistan vets are just overlooked unless somebody has an agenda or has an after-thought. It's all smoke and mirrors. Everyone is focused on the death toll whether it's too high or reasonable enough but if we look at the severely wounded and mental health issues, they are the issues that may separate this war from others. Young Warfighters are going to need long-term managed healthcare.

A vast majority of Warfighters are surviving violent trauma multiple times and completing their tours of duty with injuries unlike the past. Surviving has become an issue itself like never before; medical, financial, family, occupational and social rehabilitation needs fall short.

—I also think we'll be fucked if these issues don't get serious attention very quickly. I guess that's a Warfighter thing but it doesn't have to be. I hope as a society our veterans of Vietnam have taught us all something about taking care of our own when Warfighters return from war. Those veterans suffered through that lesson and we should all be damned if things haven't changed.

I volunteered for the war, we all did. We might bitch about some things but the majority of us would do it all again especially now that we know the real cost of failure. Most Warfighters return with a very personal sense of responsibility for the outcome of the war. Most of the injured and many of the uninjured can't help but come home completely different than before the war. Being different doesn't always necessarily mean bad, we are just different—we change. At the same time some of us are changed because we are hurt. Being hurt and losing a lot of shit because of it is an issue that we could use some more assistance with. Sorry to ask. How do Warfighters start over from scratch when at times we can't even think straight? I am not saying that in a metaphorical sense—I mean it literally, thinking is sometimes an actual problem and it makes decision making difficult. Duh!

I see young injured Warfighters every day, do you think their girlfriends/boyfriends or spouses will stay with them? Very often it's doubtful. If it was something I could bet on . . . I would bet on the break-up, get rich, and retire. Will they be relegated to only seeing their kids for four days a month? Probably. Personally, I know sometimes we all think dying would have been easier than being at a hospital month after month, losing a family, being hurt, being mad all the time and that comes straight from the Warfighters here at their most honest times. It's a lot to handle, losing a part of yourself is just one thing—losing your support system back home usually follows right behind. I don't have a good answer, I just know that one exists and I am going to try and find it. What's fair about this shit?!

The news back home so often seems out of sync with what we know to be true on the ground in Iraq. It becomes like an information blackout on things that recently meant life and death. So we can't follow anything about the world we just left and know best but we don't yet fit in the world back home either. It's a strange sort of purgatory. Not even the information age makes a difference to inform people of current war events unless the events are staged.

Everything you see on the news about the war is about three to six months old so please stop thinking you know what is happening and armchair quarterbacking; talk to a Warfighter—and stop listening to politicians and the media. I can attest to systems and operations in place that would make the best fiction writer look like an idiot, so stop being so critical of what you "think" is not happening. The comedians that make operations in Iraq look like a joke are a joke because they severely underestimate our capabilities.

Enjoy the jokes but they really are "just jokes" so don't assume the information is accurate or unbiased. For instance, if the terrorists can't really "follow us home" then how were they able to kill approximately three thousand Americans on September 11, 2001? Sometimes I want to tell people to grow the fuck up or run for political office, get elected and change shit your way, but in America, if you vote then you have a right to complain. So God love 'em—because that's partly what we are fighting for. And that's why I watch Bill Maher's show on HBO, love "The Howard Stern Radio Show," and can spend a Sunday listening to televangelist Joyce Meyer.

Nothing is perfect and if you crawl up anybody's ass long enough—you're bound to find some shit. There is a lot of sacrifice going on and we just need more support for the mission and some better training to get the job done. If listening to comedians has weight in your decision-making process then my credibility should really get through to you. Trust me, I don't deserve that kind of power—take time and learn all you can on your own.

I can't figure out why the WWII Memorial is filled with incredible inspiring speeches of intestinal fortitude and sacrifice; however, I listen to my parents' generation and so many are willing to fail in Iraq. Just like the attack on Pearl Harbor, we were still attacked on our soil on 9/11 and we didn't stop fighting in WWII until the fight was over, even though America suffered so many deaths. Today, there are a lot of severe injuries but far less casualties and young people eligible to fight are not protesting like the middle-age Americans are.

I feel cheated of support for the mission and become so angry thinking about it. I also feel like a pussy because my granddad had it so much tougher than I did. I have nothing to complain about. He was a WWII Warfighter with years and years in a POW camp who drank almost until the day he died because of it, and he never even had a fighting chance; what did I really have to complain about in Iraq—the news media—antiwar activists—political parties posturing for control and using the mission, MY mission for their purpose . . . who cares about all that? I guess I do.

I was preaching the concepts of freedom to the Iraqi people, then it hit me: understanding freedom is only the first step. The team and I were doing all we could to promote and model freedom of thought in Iraq but until they take it one step further and desire liberty unilaterally then we wasted our time. If we don't commit the time to afford them the security to discover liberty then our sacrifice has not been maximized. All this takes a lot of dedication and a willingness to win not a single battle or campaign but one ideology over another, mostly based in the non-kinetic fight.

Individual liberty over political and religious intolerance will take time. Iraq hasn't even learned to be tolerant of their own people yet and that's why they need us. If we don't help they'll grow more intolerant and America will suffer, leading to more restrictions on our own liberty here under the guise of security. Democrats and Republicans have good points of contention. Because if we stay, it hurts—if we leave, it also hurts. Pick your poison, I say we'll deal with it sooner or later so let's get it done now since we already started.

I took my dad to Capitol Hill to look around and we couldn't go into the building. I was incensed, not so much that I need to be put on a "watch list," relax please. The reason I can't go in is because of terrorism concerns, our access was limited . . . we both fought for that access and deserve it, so does every person that votes, child that will vote, foreign tourist that wants to see our government work, and every other Warfighter.

The people that set up that security policy know what they are doing and I don't second-guess them, nothing can be done locally until we win globally. What if one day every city becomes that way, where is the liberty in that? If we lose our freedom of movement then the shitheads have won because they are forcing us into a behavior that is contradictory to our core values.

I believe in "give me liberty or give me death" and I am even willing to lead a revolution or take up arms against my own government to maintain it. What is the point of living if you can't live? . . . God owns my soul and he can have it now if I can't have liberty here on Earth.

My dad and I went to a ballgame today, it's a guy thing; both Warfighters of two eras sitting together, alive and with thousands of Americans on a Sunday afternoon. He sat branded with his new tattoo and me with mine. During the seventh-inning stretch a young girl sang "God Bless America" as we all stood to show respect. I looked at the American flag and at that instant all the emotions from the war memorials here in DC flashed through me.

For the first time ever, I felt good about my service in Iraq—I didn't only see my failures. I pulled my sunglasses over my eyes to cry (only a little, so shut up) and asked my dad, "This is why I went to Iraq, right?" He answered simply, "Yep"; it was such a guy thing. In that one moment and from that three-letter word I "got it" and that was the end of it, it was a good birthday. The home team won in the ninth.

Wouldn't that make a great ending—so sweet and warm? Are you fucking kidding me, have you read the words of Boone Cutler so far or did you skip to the last chapter like I do? That was a true story and the home team did win in the ninth on my birthday but this isn't baseball and I don't write storybook endings. Reality is a constant double-edged sword and it may really suck depending on the ticket you bought. This is a war, there is no ninth inning, the home team changes every other day, and who really cares about MY birthday? Enjoy your life and every day of it because every day not behind a rifle is a good day, and every day not in front of one is great. Take your kids to a ballgame and enjoy your favorite television show, talk your shit about Britney Spears or secretly desire to be Brad Pitt and or Angelina Jolie—whatever.

But remember this; the American Military sees battlefield operations and reconciliation for peace as different situations that deserve different rules of conduct. We use deception to gain the advantage on the battlefield; however, when we negotiate we tend to lean towards reconciliation with openness by honoring our commitments. If America violates an agreement we still have a sense of disgrace over the issue; besides, it's just bad business for future opportunities. (Get off the soapbox, I know it has happened before but I am speaking in principle generalities.)

Here is the fundamental difference between EVERY MUSLIM EXTREMISTS GROUP OR LEADER and us: They see reconciliation for peace and negotiation as part of and not separate from battlefield operations; therefore, deception and dishonesty are always part of the game. There is no way to sit at a table and "work it out" because to them it is perfectly acceptable to work the angle and completely lie. There is absolutely no way to negotiate with the Muslim Extremists that are on a mission unless you simply give them everything they want. By the way, all they really want is for us to be dead. Here are three truths about the area Voodoo served in Iraq: Muqtada IS in charge of all the bullshit; there is no rogue Shia element doing the bad while Muqtada is a Shia saint; and anybody that thinks Muqtada al Sadr can be negotiated with is a damn fool.

The people telling you that Muqtada can be negotiated with know that I am telling the truth and they are lying to you. This is a foolish, hopeful ideal that will only unite control of the Muslim Extremist elements throughout the region. The Day of Judgment is the ultimate goal for Jaysh al Mehdi and their Muslim allies.

We can't blow them back to the Stone Age because that causes moderates to become extremists for survival sake, thus creating more extremists; we can't ignore them and wait for the shitheads to grow and attack us either. So the only way to deal with this is to persuade, change, and influence the population underneath the ruling faction—splinter them to turn them inside out then follow up with targeted Direct Action and support. It takes thirty years to create change and influence a new generation. Sorry but that is the reality and there is no microwave to speed up the process.

The target audience that wants us is young; they desire freedom and want the change that we have to offer—in a nutshell, they want peace, porn, and Pepsi, just like most Americans. It won't be easy and it will be a constant issue during most of our lives. Warfighters are here to stay and until our military accepts that we need more kinetic operations built around psychological operations and not the other way, we are going to be building the barriers that we are trying to break. For example; Muqtada dying would be good, us killing Muqtada would be bad because Jaysh al Mehdi would compare it to Saddam killing Muqtada's family but his people being willing to discredit him would be great. This is the new Cold War, it has been here, it is here now, and it ain't going anywhere anytime soon. We could all use a little reality check on that concept.

The Iraqi people and most Muslims I know are good people, just like you and me, and they are more similar to us than they are different.

I will always open my home to them the same as any other friend. I have learned tremendous respect and compassion from them, as much as from the good people in my country. What separates them and us are the groups like Jaysh al Mehdi that impose rule over them and strangle the life out of them—that's it.

Promote this book if you got something from it (I have to feed my kids and soon won't have a job). It would make a great gift, buy it for someone special that enjoys an easy read about an interesting subject with in depth information. Enjoy your lives every day and laugh, but don't forget to prepare for combat. Leaders, politicians, and all Americans should at least consider renewing their commitment of support for the Warfighter's mission abroad, better training at home, and better treatment for our injured for as long as it takes: Liberty or Death!

With all my sincerity and a few jokes,

Boone

"War is a mere continuation of politics by other means"
Carl von Clausewitz

"To win and engagement; be the first to process the most information accurately and immediately commit yourself with the correct fighting skills. Once victorious; become the one with the most information and commitment to winning through the influence of your ideas and your willingness to compromise or you'll lose more than just a battle."

Boone Cutler

Warfighters of any era and their family members that read this book and are too drunk, too medicated, too confused, too sober, or too angry about all the nonsense after coming home or being in combat can call for help. Contact your local Vet Center in any major city; because what you feel inside only feels unique. Vet Center services are free for you and your family. It's where we take care of our own so we can take care of each other again. Remember that we will always be one together.

If you wish to donate to help injured Warfighters, please visit www. woundedwarriorproject.org

LaVergne, TN USA
11 November 2010
204535LV00001B/130/P